CONTENTS

From DISGRACE *to* DIGNITY

REGGIE LONGCRIER

ISBN 978-1-64114-005-8 (Paperback)
ISBN 978-1-64114-006-5 (Digital)

Christian Faith Publishing, Inc.
296 Chestnut Street
Meadville, PA 16335
www.christianfaithpublishing.com

Printed in the United States of America

1

IT TAKES A VILLAGE

The Village was the first public housing in the county projects around Atlantic City, New Jersey. We had green grass, neatly manicured lawns, and neighbors could leave doors unlocked. On Saturdays, people would take pride in shining their brass doorknobs. The little girls jumped hopscotch, double dutch, and played hide and seek with the boys. The boys played marbles and scummy tops, high jumped, slap boxed, and jump the trash house roof.

The neighbors watched each another's children. We called them "nosy neighbors" because it seemed like they were always looking out the window to see what we were doing so that they could tell our parents when they got home from work. In those days, only a few of us were fortunate enough to have both parents in the home. It was typical for a neighbor to knock on the door or send one of their children to ask for a cup of sugar, a couple slices of bread, some cream, or seven cents for a loaf of bread until payday on the first of the month. A few of the more fortunate kids had fathers in the National Guard. They would leave for two weeks at a time then come back with gifts and money for their family. Their children could come to the armory with their friends, and their fathers would give them all some money. I often wondered why my daddy never joined the National Guard.

Every village had a gang. We would have occasional gang wars using our fists, sticks, bottles, and rocks. Some of us had very unique skills in rock-throwing and stick-swinging, and one kid was known for his bite. We had a street gang called the Marshall gang, which was named after the Marshall Brothers, the leaders. Some referred to this gang as the Leeds Avenue gang because of the street they lived on. Not many wanted to tangle with these guys because they had a reputation for being a bit extreme in their war tactics.

I remember one day, they caught our leader (the tallest kid in our gang), put a noose around his neck, and gathered around a big tree. It seemed like they were giving him his last rites and asking if there was anything he'd like to say before dying. I couldn't hear what he said, if anything at all. Most of us cowered behind some bushes, wishing there was something we could do to stop it. We were outnumbered and outgunned. We feared that if they caught us, we would be hung too. One of us had enough sense to slip off and get his mom and big sister. They came rushing to his rescue shouting, "Turn that boy loose! Turn that boy loose!" This was not the last hanging attempt by the Leeds Avenue gang. They tried to hang another kid named Ray who lived in one of the neighboring villages, but some grown folks intervened.

One day, Huey, the leader of the Marshall gang, decided he was going to terrorize our village, like Goliath calling out the Philistines. "Come on out. I'll fight anybody!" he shouted three times. I decided I wasn't going to hide. I wasn't going to take it. I wasn't going to let Huey punk me out so I stepped out to fight him.

I was no David that day! Huey picked me up, body-slammed me on the grass and smashed my head into a steel pole, knocking me unconscious. Then he lifted me up in his arms and carried me to my house. He knocked on the front door with both arms full of me, and told my mother with a toothless grin he had knocked me out. I don't remember all that she said to him, but it wasn't very nice.

Some days, the *wars* between the village gangs would get so bad that the neighbors would have to call Willie Clayton. He was a motorcycle cop who lived nearby. When called, he would come riding through the village with his motorcycle roaring loud. The sight of him wearing his helmet, black leather jacket, black leather boots, and gun on the side with the sound of that motorcycle would instill the fear of God in us all. When we heard him coming, we would run and hide behind a bush or a tree, or try to make it inside if we could. We would say to one another, "You better run! Here comes Willie Clayton!" Just the sound of his name would invoke fear in the toughest of us. After he rode through three or four times, gunning the motor of his cycle, he would leave, and everything would go back to normal.

I walked to the Indiana Avenue Elementary School four blocks from the village. Every day after school, I walked from the schoolyard to an alley street that led to the YMCA on the corner. We had two YMCAs in the city, one on the south side for white folks and one on the north side for black folks. While other boys my age would play basketball, lift weights, do somersaults, and race around, I was practicing my pool game on one of the three or four tables they had. Every day, I would rush to get on a table to play, sometimes beating older boys there from junior high school and high school. I took to pool like a fish to water. Before long, I was competing with many of the older guys, playing twenty-five- and fifty-point games. In no time, I earned a pretty good reputation among the older boys who played along with a name I wasn't partial to—Juice. Mr. Boyd, the director of the YMCA, gave me this name because while noticing my skills at the pool table, he saw that I had a bad habit of slobbering and wiping it with my sleeve. One day, after finishing my shot with everyone watching and admiring my skills on the table for a sixth grader, I found myself unconsciously slobbering. Mr. Boyd noticed along with everyone else. "Hey, he's slobbering! Juice Lips! That's what we'll call you!" It would be many years before I could shake that handle, especially since Mr. Boyd gave it to me. Talk about the luck of the draw. Of all the handles in the world, mine had to be Juice. To make matters worse, Mr. Boyd, as an adult, would say it in such a derogatory manner, "Juice Lips." The other boys were a little merciful and kept it short by just calling me "Juice." It would be almost 10 years before people would stop calling me that.

I remember going to visit a woman I was dating when I was well past twenty-one years old. At that time, most people never knew my real name. She had been telling her brother about me and that she wanted him to meet Reggie. When he came into the room and saw me, he turned to her and said, "Oh, I know Juice!" After all these years, he still thought people were calling me Juice. I didn't tell him any different. I just grinned and took it in stride.

2

SHOE SHINE BOY

"You can't look neat when your shoes are beat! You can't look neat when your shoes are beat! Shine, sir? Shine, sir? Shoeshine, sir?" That was the chant of the little boys who made their hustle shining shoes in the bars and nightclubs and Atlantic City's seven-mile stretch of boardwalk. I hustled newspapers and sold flower seeds then I decided it was time to get a shoeshine box to help make ends meet.

After several weeks of working the streets on the boardwalks of Atlantic City, I discovered the other little boys my age who had the same idea. As we became friends, we shared our best hustling spots with one another. Before long, we had a shared directory of nightclubs, bars, and boardwalk streets along with the best times to be there to make the most money. Our hustle was suddenly hindered by an ordinance that passed prohibiting the little shoeshine boys from shining shoes on the boardwalk because they were becoming a nuisance to the tourists. I remember the NAACP getting involved and going to bat for us. My friend Corky and I were chosen to be the poster children of the ban. Our picture was in the newspaper wearing NAACP T-shirts while sitting with our shoeshine boxes. The caption read "Shoeshine boys banned from boardwalk because shining shoes is a nuisance to tourists. Where will they go?" After that, we began concentrating our efforts in the clubs and bars, shining the shoes of pimps, hustlers, and gangsters. Some clubs would not allow us in so we just worked the outside. The shoeshine boys bonded closer. We became more creative, stepping up our act, even entertaining a customer with a song if requested. I just sang backup and sometimes danced. Sometimes tips would be so big we could almost smell them coming!

On Sunday mornings, we would be up early enough to work the breakfast show at the infamous Club Harlem where we would shine the shoes of celebrities like Sammy Davis Jr., Slappy White, and others. We would shine the shoes of the great pimps and hustlers who drove long, pretty cars and walked with the most beautiful women in the world. They all wore jewelry designed to sparkle and draw attention. During this time, I made up my mind what I wanted to be—just like those guys! They seemed to have no problems with making ends meet, sailing through life with the greatest of ease and having the most fun doing it. I would learn the morals and values of the criminal subculture from the pimps and hustlers I admired. They soon became my teachers and textbooks as I went through the school of life.

After the breakfast show on Sunday mornings, I would go to my father's shoeshine shop, which was really a front for gambling and liquor sales that took place in the back. I was allowed to work with Old Man Rock who made his money in the front shining shoes. People would stop in on their way to church or on their way back to get a shine. Pool hustlers and gamblers would also stop in for a shine just because it was Sunday. They often wore ties and suits but they never went to church. My father paid somebody in law enforcement to let him know when the Feds were in town or just what was going down. One time, Old Man Rock forgot to tell my father that someone came by the shop to inform my father that the Feds would be in town next week, warning him not to open the back. Rock forgot all about it until the Feds came in that week. They took my father, Rock, and everyone in the back to jail. While in the jail cell with my father, Rock remembered and said, "Richard, I forgot to tell you that they said you were not supposed to open the back this week because the Feds were in town!"

By the time I was in seventh grade in junior high, my uncle Bill was taking me to the pool halls in Atlantic City: Bruce's, Brodie's, Gibson, Herb's, and the Golden Cue. He was a pool hustler of sorts, moonlighting at Atlantic City's Claridge Hotel as a cook and raising two daughters. He always kept a pocket full of quarters. When we were small, he'd give each of us a big fat quarter—sometimes two—which was a lot for a little kid in those days. He would always wear a suit and tie, and his motto was "I'm Boardwalk Bill, dressed to kill, never worked and never will."

Uncle Bill would take me to the pool halls even though I was too young to play on the tables. Sometimes the houseman would allow me to shoot a game because I was Boardwalk Bill's nephew and I played well for my age without tearing up the tables. Uncle Bill would give me a different pointer or lesson in pool every week but no matter how good I became, I was never good enough to impress him. If he was ever impressed, he never showed it. Perhaps his game was so superior to mine he never even noticed. Later, I started going to the pool halls without him. Even though I was still underage, they never said anything, except maybe give a nod and say, "That's Boardwalk's nephew." Before long, I was playing six-ball, nine-ball, points, and pockets apiece for money as I had seen my uncle Bill do in times past. I became known in all of the pool halls in Atlantic City as the young kid that had a good stick. Sometimes I won; sometimes I lost. But most of the time, I won as long as I stayed in my class.

3

FROM DETENTION TO REFORMATORY

Shining shoes and playing pool got to be old and too slow for the money. My crew and I graduated to purse-snatching, shoplifting, and breaking and entering.

It wasn't long before I made my second resident visit to the Egg Harbor Detention Home for Boys after breaking into a men's clothing store. I shared a room with a fat, white kid named Stan. At night when the lights were out and everybody was supposed to be in bed sleeping, Stan and I would entertain ourselves by throwing checkers at the jar that was used as our night urinal. All the rooms had one. One night while throwing checkers, laughing, and making a lot of noise, the night officer turned on the lights and caught me up before I could get back to my bed. He escorted me to a large restroom down the hall and put me in a cell-like cage. It was used as a sort of time out for boys who would misbehave or get out of control.

Later that night, Mr. Kerry, the superintendent, came over to pay me a visit. He said that his officer called and woke him from his sleep. Still wearing his pajamas, he opened the cage-like door, came in, and stepped on my feet. He weighed every bit of three hundred pounds and beat me like no child should ever be beat. I never told my parents but the other little boys all knew about it. After spending several days in that cage, I found out that Mrs. Kerry convinced Mr. Kerry to let me out on Christmas Eve so that I could come downstairs and eat with the other little boys. My forearms and back were bruised from the beating. Later that evening after dinner with the other little boys, we stood in the living room of the detention home with noses pressed against the window. We watched and listened to a church group that came by to sing Christmas carols to us while out sleigh-riding.

After a month or so in the detention home, it wasn't long before I entered the state reformatory for boys called Jamesburg. Our van pulled on to the grounds with ten to twelve other boys. Some of them had been there before while others were coming for the first time. Older boys told me what to expect. "Don't let nobody change you. Be ready to fight. Don't be a chump or back down. Don't let nobody tap you on your behind."

At Jamesburg, grass was neatly manicured and gave the appearance of a college campus. Everything we needed to sustain ourselves was produced right there on the grounds. We had farms, dairies, piggeries, poultry houses, workshops, and a commissary. I was in another world. We lived in three-story buildings called cottages, and there were around twelve cottages on the campus. They were designated for junior, intermediate, or senior residents. The cottage mother and father lived on the top floor. A large dormitory for fifty to sixty boys was on the middle floor along with a TV, living room, and library. In the basement were lockers lining the walls. This is where we kept our uniforms, underwear, towels, and other personal stuff. The restroom was large with toilets on one side and showers on the other. Reception cottage was where all of the new kids would go upon arrival to Jamesburg.

Kids stayed in reception for three to four weeks until they had gotten all of their shots and had been seen by a doctor. It seemed like we each took a million evaluation tests in reception. Every Thursday and Friday, new kids would arrive from cities such as Newark, Jersey City, Atlantic City, Camden, Patterson, and other cities throughout the state.

At night before going upstairs to watch TV, Mr. Avery would make us do knee bends until we were sore. Up, down, up down, up down. Then with all the boys lined along the basement wall, he would start his initiation of the new boys that had come in that week. This was done mostly on Friday night. He would approach each new kid one by one. "Where you from, son?" he would ask.

"Patterson, sir," a boy would reply.

"What you in here for?"

"I snatched a pocketbook," the boy would say.

"Why, boy, that was my mother's pocketbook, you son of a B!" He would commence beating the kid with his fist and kicking him as if he was trying to kick a field goal. Then he would move down the line to the next new kid. "What you in for, son?"

"Breaking in a gas station."

"Where you from?"

"Newark."

"You son of a B, that was my brother's gas station you broke in!" Then he would commence to beating the kid, sometimes drawing blood. As we watched him move down the line with eyes bloodshot, we knew this man was deranged. However, there was no one to stop this fool as he would continue this charade. "What's your name, son? Where are you from? What you in for? What? Stealing a car? Boy, that was my cousin's car!" Then the beatdown came. When we finally got upstairs to the TV room to watch a little TV before bedtime, Mr. Avery would sometimes be sitting at his desk surveying the room. Then out of nowhere, he would start throwing chairs, saying, "I'm tired of y'all. I'm tired of looking at you. It's time to go to bed. Everybody outta here!" I don't believe Mr. Avery liked anybody, not even himself.

In the center of the basement floor in each cottage was a drain. Large benches surrounded the drain and formed the shape of a boxing ring. We sat on the benches changing clothes; playing checkers, cards, and other activities in between school or work detail; or while waiting to go to chow hall. The basement was the place where vicious fights would be carried out under the watchful eye of a cottage officer who would sit at his desk at the entrance. Young inmates would gather around a fight to root for their homeboy to win. Others called booty bandits would shout from outside the ring, "The first one to get knocked out gets done!" Some of the cottage officers would allow the boys to fight up until they called us for work detail or chow time. When we returned, we would pick up the fighting again. Sometimes you would find yourself fighting the same guy three or four days in a row because to concede meant you were weak.

Our school was named after somebody named Wilson. Some of us attended school half a day and did work half a day. I don't remember learning anything in school. Most of the boys practiced Islam. We studied and recited our lessons in the evenings while the others watched TV before bedtime. We were part of what was called the First Resurrection and learned things like the history of the hog. Some bigheaded scientist one day did some hocus-pocus with the sperm of a cat, a rat, and a dog to create the hog. That's why when you look at it, you see it has the eyes of a cat, the hair of a dog, and the tail of a rat.

Those of us professing Islam did not eat pork, among other things. The food was hazardous to your health. It was not unusual to find insects such as cockroaches, caterpillars, worms, and beetles in our chow. It helped to have a homeboy or two in the kitchen to tell you what was okay to eat and what was not. Sometimes someone would throw a dead rat or mouse in a pot of beans. It was good to have somebody to pull your coat about what was happening with the food. While most of the guys in my cottage didn't eat pork, some didn't care. We would swap our pork for their vegetables or fruit. I traded with a giant of a kid who would eat everything he could get his hands on. He was the biggest kid in the cottage. He had gorilla-like features with broad shoulders, black as night, little beady eyes, overlapping eyebrows, and big forehead. Everyone called him "the Galubarator." This was the name Mr. Turner, one of the cottage officers, had given him because of his size.

Once I left reception, I went to cottage twelve, an intermediate cottage that had mostly older white boys who couldn't make it in the senior cottages eight and three. I resented them for putting me there. I felt they were cramping my style. Although I was the shortest kid in the cottage, I still felt my hand called for one of the senior cottages where the action was. So I made up my mind that I was going to have to do something really crazy for them to ship me to one of the senior cottages like hit somebody upside the head with a deck brush or a mop ringer. I began plotting my transfer, but there was a transfer already being hatched—one I had not planned. I had only been a week on a job that I didn't like.

I was working in poultry, taking eggs from a chicken coup and feeding the chickens. I heard, "Longcrier, report to the detail office right away." Upon arriving at the detail office, I ran into another kid named Patterson who was in reception with me. "What you doing here?" we said to each other. Looking out of the window of Mr. Dixon's office was a kid we both knew from reception. He was a big kid who went on bad. We had pulled a coat job on him in reception, leaving him with a broken jaw and a couple of cracked ribs.

"You boys come in here. Do you know Roy?" Mr. Dixon asked us. "Yes, sir, from reception," we said. "Roy, tell them what you told us." The big kid said, "Well, Patterson grabbed me and threw me in the broom closet. Longcrier threw a coat over my head. Patterson kicked me and broke my ribs. Longcrier broke my jaw, sir."

I got a transfer to do ninety days in the guidance unit. This was a unit of single cells for the bad boys, away from the population. You stayed locked up twenty-four hours a day, and you were let out for showers every three days. During that time, you could trade comic books with other boys. When I got out of GU, I was wearing an afro long before it was fashionable to do so. After doing my time, I was transferred to cottage eight. This was one of two senior cottages with a reputation for being one of the roughest stops in the institution.

My job assignment now was in the piggery, as they called it. I was to feed the pigs the leftover slop from the inmate dining hall. I not only fed the pigs, but it was my job to hose down and clean the waste from the pig pens. Every now and then, if a pig went astray into the corn field, I was the one sent to bring him back to justice. There was one hog in particular that we called Big Butch. He was the bull hog and the boss hog of the piggery. He had a reputation for being dangerous, a killer, and quick to attack. I never understood why they kept Butch around so long without taking him to slaughter. When I wasn't working the piggery, I'd be in the field lifting bales of hay and stacking them on a flatbed truck six feet high all day.

Some Saturdays we were asked to volunteer to go to one of the official's farms and help get their hay in. This was usually an all-day job. We really didn't mind because it took us off the grounds of the reformatory, and we knew that at the end of the day, we'd get a home-cooked meal, which would be prepared by the official's wife.

4

NEW YORK

When I left Jamesburg, I was on parole. The conditions of my parole were to stay away from other parolees, dishonest people, pool halls, bars, and illegal activities and seek gainful employment. I was supposed to report once a month. I broke every condition of my parole from day one, hands down. I went back to Bruce's Pool Room to continue to build a resume for crime and a recipe for disaster. I would hustle pool, cards, worthless checks, stolen property, drugs, and girls. I was addicted to the lifestyle long before I was addicted to the drugs.

Bruce's Pool Hall was the hustler's home. It was a breeding ground for pimps, pool hustlers, pickpockets, card sharks, con men, and professional dice throwers. The characters that frequented Bruce's had funny names like Poor Boy, Paper Boy, Fats, Blood, Smoke, Red, Yellow, Little George, Interstate George, Fast Sam, and Fast Black. Numbers were being played and written, prostitutes would check in with their pimps, hustlers would await their prey, and crooked cops would pick up their cut. For convenience, there was a criminal attorney with an office in the building in case you caught a case. In Bruce's, shady characters were regulars.

Other characters were there sitting around, ready to sell you their latest get-rich scheme.

One day while sitting around shooting the breeze with my childhood friend and partner DD, a junkie name Crowbar Shorty approached us. He asked if we wanted to make some money. "Y'all thinking you're getting some money now? Y'all ain't seen no money until you start getting some dope money. Y'all could take that money you been making around here and parlay it into a fortune."

It wasn't long before Crowbar Shorty talked us into letting him take us to New York to buy a dope package to bring back to Atlantic City to sell. Once we arrived in New York, we got off the bus and he gave us strict instructions to stay close to him and keep up. Crowbar walked quickly through the port authority with us close behind. We were trying to catch a subway train uptown to Harlem. We got off the train at 116th Street and Lennox Avenue. Crowbar instructed us again to stay close while he weaved in and out of the crowds, asking people here and there about who had the best dope out. He bought dope from several dealers and took it to a nearby shooting gallery to test so we would know which was the best package to take back and sell. D.D. and I sat around the gallery and watched Crowbar test the dope, one bag after another. He feverishly poked needles full of dope in the rope-like veins in his arm and then we would have to watch him nod for what seemed like an hour before he would decide which dope was best.

One time, Crowbar suggested we try a taste of dope just in case he was not around and we needed to buy some so we would know what to look for. At the time, it sounded like a reasonable idea. All bad ideas sound good at first. I thought, *What could it hurt to try it?* If I just did it one time, I wouldn't get strung out like Crowbar. I wouldn't need it every day. I was too strong and too smart for that to happen to me so I allowed Crowbar to give me my first shot of heroin. I watched him draw a small amount of dope into a syringe. He pinched the fatty part of my upper right arm and inserted the needle. This was called skin popping. It took ten to fifteen minutes to feel the effects of the dope this way versus mainlining into a vein, which was the way Crowbar used his drugs. Within a few minutes, I began to feel the effects of the heroin. I didn't like how it made me feel and it made me vomit. I knew then I would never become strung out on this stuff like the many junkies I saw on the street corners of Harlem and Atlantic City.

D.D. was adamant about not trying it because he saw what heroin did to his father. His father had been in and out of jail while we were kids. His father would get out of jail and soon go back to using heroin again. D.D. knew firsthand the strain heroin put on his family and their father-son relationship. Looking back, D.D. was not that passionate about selling drugs either. I think he just wanted to have dope on hand, hoping it would draw his father to him for a relationship they never had.

Once we got back to Atlantic City, we gave Crowbar some of the dope to sell while we waited on him in the pool room because we were too young to be in the bar on the corner where he was selling the dope. We didn't get rich like we thought we would. We learned that Crowbar just wanted a means of getting high rather than get rich. At the time, we didn't know any better than trusting a junkie to sell dope. Although we did make a little money with Crowbar selling our dope, it was never enough for us to think we would ever get rich. Trusting a drug addict to sell dope was just as bad as trusting a monkey to sell bananas. It was a disaster. After a few more trips to New York with Crowbar, we decided we would get out of the dope game. We would just use it as a side business when other hustles got slow, especially in winter.

After that, we never sold drugs exclusively. It was always in combination with other hustles.

Bruce's pool room seemed to be the only classroom where I felt worthy to compete because I always failed miserably in academics. While I was failing in the classroom, I was making up for it in the pool room. My ability to throw dice to insure I would make my number made up for my inability to know my numbers in class. My ability to run the balls on a pool table or deal cards in a way that I was sure to win made up for my inability to keep up with the rest of the class in school. In the pool room, I always got high marks for my pool game. In the pool room, I didn't have an attention deficit. I always paid attention. I always studied hard in craps, pool, cards, and con. I studied and loved all my subjects. I took my lessons home to study and brought them back the next day, eager and ready to learn more. I never needed to lie and say the dog ate my homework.

By the time I turned seventeen, I felt I was ready to take my act on the road. I needed a bigger playground. I planned and saved all that summer to go to New York with Josh Wash, who lived and hustled in New York for many years. He was back in Atlantic City, down on his luck. He promised me that after Labor Day, we would leave together for New York and share the expenses. The night before we were to leave, it was a Sunday night and the action was slow in Brodie's Pool Room. Two of the four tables were occupied and the other two were dark with no action. Ready shooters sat along the sidelines, watching one of the two games that were being played and occasionally watching the door to see who would come in to play a game for money.

While Josh and I were sitting there discussing our trip the following day, in walks Little George. Josh said, "How about a game of one pocket for ten dollars a game?"

Little George answered, "Naw, but I'll play you some points if you give me five balls going to twenty-five."

They haggled back and forth until they decided on a game of nine-ball, giving Josh all the breaks. Within a few hours, Josh was broke and Little George was talking smack. Josh broke his pool stick in disgust. After Josh finished cussing himself out, he turned to Little George and asked for a little money to hustle with. This was not unusual among gentlemen pool players. Little George threw a twenty-dollar bill across the table to Josh and made his exit. Josh then turned to me and said, "Let's go around the corner to Kelley's and get something to eat." Kelley's had the best fried chicken in town. While waiting for our order, I asked Josh if he was still going to New York with me the next day. He looked at me and said, "Man, I don't have no money to be going to New York now."

I said, "Man, you can't back out on me now. Look, I'll pay your way and you pay me back." He said no. I was crushed. I saved about eight hundred dollars but I didn't tell him that. I couldn't back out now. I already told everybody that I was leaving. I put a lot of work into convincing my mother I was ready. There was no way I was going to undo that. With bags in hand, I was on my way to New York by bus the next day. After having arrived at the Port Authority station, I found my way to the A-train straight to Harlem with one lead in my pocket. It was the address of Cody, a pool hall rat who had been living between Atlantic City and New York for years.

He gave me his address sometime the year before in the pool hall and said "If you're ever in New York, look me up." Well, here I was.

Cody lived at 2340 Seventh Avenue, next to a little restaurant-coffee shop called the Sugar Bowl. At first, I slept on the floor of Nick Nac and Reese's apartment in the building where Cody lived. They were both singers and dancers who were from Atlantic City but living in New York, waiting for their big break. These guys helped Cody when he first got to the city. Now they were helping me until I found a room.

Before the week was out, I had found a room on 126th Street between Fifth and Lennox for forty dollars a week. I thought this would be ideal because there was a pool room around the corner on 125th Street at the top of the Four Roses bar. Although the room had bed bugs and roaches, I somehow made it work until I could do better. My dream to make it in New York on my pool game alone had turned into a nightmare after losing all my money to a seasoned pool hustler named Yellow one night. Now here I was, seventeen years old, broke, and hungry in Harlem with no one to turn to except to take up with a couple of street thugs who made their living by mugging people late at night.

During the day, I took up with an old junkie named Willie who taught me how to shoplift, stealing boxes and bundles of clothes from the garment district downtown. Before long, I acquired a nice little bankroll, and the timing couldn't be better. A room just became open in the building where Cody stayed. There was even another pool hall on Seventh Avenue between 138th and 139th Streets where I would meet Fifth Avenue Red. He tried to encourage me to go back to school and always downplayed the hustle despite his reputation for being a street genius.

I would meet up with Willie most mornings at about eight at the Japanese restaurant where we would have breakfast before going out to hustle. One morning, I had placed my order and was waiting on Willie. He walked in, eyes red and nose runny, with some news that I was not prepared for. "Young Blood," as he called me, "I don't think I'm going out today. I'm sick."

"What do you mean sick?" I asked.

"Blood, I can't go out there sick like this. I got to get my sickness off. I need me some dope."

I didn't want to go downtown by myself so I asked him how much he needed to take his sickness off. In those days, you could get heroin for two dollars a bag and fifteen bags or half a load for thirty dollars—twenty-eight if you copped short. I gave him twenty-three dollars to go with the five-dollar loan he had. With that, he could get a half load. I followed Willie around the corner and upstairs to a third floor apartment called a shooting gallery. This was a place where junkies went to rent their needles for a dollar or paid a price to use their drugs without interruption. In the shooting gallery, people who called themselves "doctors" would sit around waiting for someone who was in need of their talent to find a vein in any part of their body. They could insert a needle with precision without wasting a drop of dope. This gallery was also where Willie slept on a couch at night. Even though the house man was his homeboy, he wasn't cutting Willie any slack. He had to support his habit the best he could.

The dope man happened to be camping out in the gallery that morning, making a few sales here and there. People came through on their way to work and getting their morning shot before going out. Willie spoke to a man nodding in the corner. "Sam, you still got some dope left?"

"Yeah. What you want, Willie?" said the dope man.

"I've got twenty-eight. I need a half a load. I'm sick, man. I'll tighten you later when I get in." Sam tossed Willie fifteen bags wrapped in a rubber band. Willie handed him the money. Sam was another one of Willie's homeboys. They always looked out for one another. As Willie began to prepare his dope in a mayonnaise jar top, he turned to me and said, "You want a shot of this dope, Young Blood?"

At that moment it seemed that the silence that followed was heavy, waiting for my response. A prostitute sat in a chair with a needle hanging from her thigh. A man was on the couch with a needle in his armpit. Another man was holding a small mirror in one hand with a needle in the other, trying to pinch his jugular vein. Some sat just nodding while others were either coming in or going out. Although the gallery was quite busy that morning, it was not too busy for all to stop and see how I would respond to the offer that had been made to me. I didn't want everybody to think I was square so I yielded to a G-shot. This was the smallest amount of dope you could take next to asking for the cotton. I asked one of the doctors sitting around to hit me. He asked for my left arm and drew up a small amount of dope in a syringe. Tying my arm and finding a vein, he quickly inserted the needle into my armpit. I watched the blood shoot up into the syringe. I entered into a state of euphoria then it was cloud nine and on into outer darkness.

I couldn't see; I couldn't move. I knew that I had gone further than I wanted to go. I overdosed. I heard people talking but I couldn't move. I heard somebody say, "Who brought this young kid in here?"

Another said, "Somebody get him out of here!" I still couldn't move or see.

Somebody else said, "Let's put this kid on the roof. He's gonna draw heat on the building." My mind sent a signal for my arms to rise in protest, but my arms couldn't move. My mind sent a signal to my feet to stomp in protest but my feet couldn't move.

By this time, a deep voice behind me said, "When I'm through with my shot, I'll help y'all lift this kid to the roof." Then for the first time, I heard Willie's voice as if he had just come out of a nod saying, "I can't let y'all do that to this kid. Blood is with me."

The next thing I knew, I was standing outside of the building with Willie putting snow down my back and around my forehead. Realizing that I just came back from an overdose, I hugged Willie and kissed him all over his face, thanking him for having revived me. I vowed that I would never do that again. That was, until months later when I ran into Dairy Boy on 125th Street.

He was another pool hustler who used to hang out in Gibson's Pool Hall back home. Dairy Boy had just gotten out of Rikers Island. Along with being a pool hustler, he got hooked on heroin and was looking for a fix. I was so glad to see a familiar face from home that I forgot all about the vow I made months before. I decided to buy some dope to celebrate Dairy Boy's homecoming. After having copped, we hopped on the number two train downtown to the Village where Dairy Boy had a small apartment. Pulling out two sets of gimmicks and handing me one, he asked, "Can you hit yourself?"

"Naw, you got to hit me." Once he finished his shot, he attended to me. "I don't need much, just a little," I said. Dairy Boy liked to mix cocaine with heroin.

"Have you ever had a speedball?"

Once again, not wanting to appear square, I said, "Yeah, I've done a speedball before. I just want a little though because this is your party. I just need you to hit me." I watched the blood shoot up into the syringe, hanging out of my arm. Then I felt my legs give way from under me while feeling somewhat euphoric. I overdosed again!

Dairy Boy revived me but he didn't seem as concerned about my overdose as he was about his woman coming home from work and catching me there. As he was putting me out of the apartment, he was quick to remind me that Coon was coming home from Rikers Island next week and that we needed to get together to celebrate his homecoming too.

5

BACK IN ATLANTIC CITY
ONE YEAR LATER

One year later, I was back in Atlantic City. I was hardened by New York and armed with a few more tricks up my sleeve. I spent most of my time hustling fake jewelry, pool, cards, and dice. Occasionally, I would get with a cat burglar named Stonehead. He always had passkeys to some of the major hotels in the city and was very meticulous and professional. You had to have soft, rubber-soled shoes and dark clothing and be ready to strike between two and three in the morning while people were asleep.

I'll never forget going out one night with Stonehead. He opened the room door as he always did—soft, easy, and quiet. If the hotel guest woke up, he would stumble and stagger, singing a song and pretending to be a drunken man who had just entered the wrong room. Stonehead always liked his marks to be asleep in the room when he got there. On this particular night, I followed Stonehead into a suite where the guests had two adjoining rooms. We saw five beds with one guy fast asleep and snoring. The others were still out of their rooms, probably partying somewhere. Stonehead quickly removed the money and credit cards from a billfold that had been lying on the nightstand. Thinking that our business was finished since the others were not in yet, I headed toward the door. Suddenly, I felt a tug on my jacket. When I turned around, Stonehead had a defiant grimace on his face as he pointed to one of the empty beds and motioned for me to get underneath it. Then he pointed to another bed that he would get underneath so we could wait for the others to come in and go to sleep to get their money too. It seemed like we waited hours for the others to come in. In the meantime, I kept thinking of the enormous risk we were taking. We might get caught! I thought, *Stonehead takes this stuff too serious. He must be crazy.* This would be the last time I would ever go out with Stonehead again. I should have known he was crazy and greedy.

Another time we were together, he climbed on to a third-floor hotel balcony where a sliding glass door was ajar and a woman was sleeping. I waited downstairs in the parking lot to play chicky. I could see Stonehead moving around in the room from the parking lot. As he was leaving the room with a camera, jewelry, and money in hand, I watched him turn back as if he had an afterthought. He noticed a large diamond ring on the sleeping woman's finger. Stonehead turned back to try to ease this ring off her finger while she was asleep. I couldn't believe it! He was having trouble getting the ring off so he decided to wet her fingers to loosen the ring so it would come off. Suddenly, the woman wakes up to see Stonehead standing over her and trying to take her ring off. She began to scream. It was a very close call.

Until this day, no matter what hotel I stay in, I always put all of the locks, chains, and latches on the door and sleep with my wallet inside my pillow because I never know what hotel Stonehead might be working.

Since I wasn't cut out to be a cat burglar, I spent most of my time perfecting the softer hustles and exchanging or practicing new moves with other hustlers in cards and craps. My pool game was always steady and reliable, drawing the attention of a prostitute named San who would come through two or three times a night looking for her pimp to give him some money. Sometimes if he wasn't there, she would wait for him and watch me play.

She came in once while her man and I had been playing six-ball for ten dollars a game. For a while, I was winning and just about got him broke. I watched him turn to her for more money to continue playing. It wasn't long before he was completely broke. Days later, I learned that she fired him not because he had lost to me, but because he had been spending most of her money on heroin since he was a heroin addict. She continued to come through some nights to watch me play. I heard through the rumor mill that she kind of liked me but I didn't put much stock in it since I was much younger than she was. I didn't think I had enough game or experience to hold on to her. Even so, she came through one night and said that she wanted to take me to breakfast at Stanley's when she was through working that morning about five thirty.

Stanley's was a restaurant where the hustlers and ladies of the night would eat breakfast before turning in for the morning. Most of the ladies would come out about seven o'clock or later and work the track until between five to seven in the morning. After having several breakfast conversations and then parting, San began bringing me gifts of clothing to the pool room before going out to work. Sometimes it would be a couple of pairs of expensive slacks and shirts to match. At other times, she gave me some type of expensive leather or suede jacket. This went on for some time until she eventually started giving me the money she'd make and keeping some to take care of the light chippy (addiction) she had acquired while in the company of the pimp she had. Before long, San suggested that we get a place together since she was now giving me all of her money.

We moved uptown to a hotel where most of the people who were making money lived. Most evenings, we would leave around the same time, usually by cab. She would go to the Bala Bar on the corner of North Carolina and Arctic where most of the ladies would stand or walk along with some slick sissies who would occasionally dress in drag, competing for the same dollar. Within a two-block radius, there would be a steady flow of traffic between New Orleans, Bala Bars, and the Carver Hotel where the ladies would turn their tricks.

In the meantime, I would be making my rounds in the pool rooms playing craps, pool, and cards. I would hang out with friends smoking weed, sharing a line from Omar Khayyam, or reciting some lines from Lawrence Harvey's *This is My Beloved*. Most of the young hustlers of my era took pride in being versed in poetry, prose, philosophy, psychology, and folklore. By this time, I was versed in John Scarne's book on cards and his other book on dice. John Scarne was reported to be one of the greatest cheats in the world. Rumor had it that Scarne was the one who broke the cheat to the government and that he had been invited to teach soldiers how to avoid being cheated.

I would usually check on San at about two in the morning. We would usually go for coffee and doughnuts while she'd tell me how her night was going. I would then turn in for the night and then wait for her to come in, which was usually about six, depending on whether or not she had made her quota for the night. Sometimes she would come in sooner, sometimes later.

As time went on, I found myself spending less time in the pool rooms and more time up the street between the New Orleans and Bala where most of the players hung out while they waited to keep a better watch on their women. Although I was too young to be in the bar, I would occasionally try to slip in. I was always run out by the bartender until one night an older pimp took up for me. He had taken a liking to me because of my pool game, and he was friends with San. He said, "Hey, why don't you leave that kid alone. If he's old enough for a woman to pay, he should be old enough for you to let him stay."

After some thought, the bartender called me over and asked, "Look kid, is Richard your daddy?"

"Yes, sir," I said.

"They tell me San is your woman," he said.

"Yes, sir," I replied.

He said, "Give me twenty." I turned and looked at the pimp for approval. He gave a nod indicating that it was okay. I pulled off a twenty-dollar bill and gave it to the bartender. He said it was all right for me to start coming in but I couldn't sit at the bar. He explained that if the police came in and found me at the bar, he would get into trouble. So for the next year or so, I would just hang around the jukebox feeding it quarters while sipping on a rum and coke, which I would pay someone to order for me from the bar while listening to Tyrone Davis' "Baby Let Me Change Your Mind." I was feeling pretty good about myself and the bankroll I had in my pocket while most people my age weren't doing as well. That is, with the exception of a chippy (addiction) that I had now acquired from snorting or skin popping a little heroin that I would sell at times just to keep a steady flow of money when hustling was slow, usually in the winter. Heroin was taboo among most pool hall hustlers, especially if you got on the needle. Hustlers would sort of blackball you, stiff-arm you, or have nothing to do with you. Most of the hustlers during that time wouldn't even use cocaine, except on rare occasions they would snort it.

One month, there was such a high grade of heroin on the streets that it had taken the lives of two of my friends. One was Louis who would only dip and dab on the weekends. His mother was sick in the hospital the night Louis overdosed, and friends tried to revive him to no avail. The police were called, the ambulance came, but no one was able to bring Louis back to life from his heroin overdose. No one was to tell Louis' mother in the hospital that her son had an overdose of heroin that night and died. People feared that she would take a turn for the worse if she found out. However, someone felt that it was their duty to break this news to her. When she heard it, she died that night in her hospital bed. The news was too unbearable for her to hear. You would think that things couldn't get any worse than that but after Louis' father heard the news of his son's overdose, he went to the hospital to be by his wife's side only to find out that she passed away also. Having heard the news about his son and now with his wife gone, Louis' father had a heart attack that same night and died. This left only Louis' young sister as the sole survivor to mourn their passing. Word spread throughout the city of how heroin destroyed this family all in one night. While some gathered to talk about the tragedy, others gathered to ask where they could buy some of this dope. Nobody but an addict would ask where to buy dope that was killing folks!

That next week, another friend of mine named Paperboy overdosed. He got the name Paperboy from delivering newspapers when he was younger, which hadn't been that long ago since he was only a year or two older than me. We heard that he loved money so much he was still delivering papers while hustling pool, craps, cards, and lending money for fifty cents on the dollar. Paperboy never got high on anything except money. He would always hang around the pool rooms or skin joints, ready to lend fifty cents on a dollar to hustlers needing his services.

One night, a slick-talking hustler with a girly voice named Blood introduced Paperboy to a hot, sultry prostitute by the name of Miss Chocolate even though her complexion was more like caramel or peanut brittle. She was one of the most beautiful women I had ever seen. To look at her, you wouldn't believe she was on the needle. People said that the three of them were together the night Paperboy took his first shot of heroin and died. Some blamed Blood, others blamed Miss Chocolate. Nobody really knew who was to blame. All we knew was that Paperboy was dead from a heroin overdose.

6

CHANGES

About a couple of months later while waiting for San to come in, I dozed off and woke up a little after 7:30 a.m. San had not gotten in yet. I sensed that something had to be wrong because she was usually in by this time. A hundred thoughts ran through my mind. Maybe she had gotten busted last night. Maybe another pimp stole her, which wasn't unusual or even worse. Maybe some sick John kidnapped her and did something to her.

I showered, got dressed, and went to look for her. I asked some of the girls who were on the track that morning if they had seen her. Most said that they saw her during the early part of the night but it seemed that no one had seen her since eight last night. I went back to my spot, thinking she might have come in while I was gone, but there was no such luck. I sat there on the edge of the bed, puzzled. I eventually dozed off and woke up to a knock on the door. "Who is it?" I said. "It's me," was the answer.

D.D. was my best friend. We had been friends since sixth grade when we used to snatch pocketbooks together. Now we hustled pool and sold fake jewelry. We occasionally chipped in to buy some dope to sell when money was slow.

We were even sent to the reformatory together about three years before for breaking into a men's clothing store on the boardwalk and taking over thirty-five thousand's worth of merchandise. There were four of us, but D. D. and I ended up taking the weight of it. We were both being sentenced to a five year in Jamesburg Reformatory for Boys.

I got up and let D.D. in the room. He walked in with a strange look on his face with a newspaper in his hand. I said, "What's up?"

He said, "Man, have you read today's paper?"

"Naw, why?"

"Man you ain't going to believe this but your girl is turning state's evidence on J. It's all right here in the paper. Read it. Man, this stuff is all over town. What you gonna do?" When I read that she would be a witness for the state, I was devastated. I was no good after that.

"What you gonna do, man? Your rep is on the line," D.D. said.

All I could say was, "I've got to cut her loose. I don't have a choice. I don't even want to talk to her, let alone see her."

D.D. was satisfied with that answer and said, "Well, man, I'm headed to Bruce's. I'll see you when you come out."

I came out that evening at eight. I decided that I wouldn't waste any time in Bala or New Orleans bars where I became accustomed to hanging because I was too ashamed. I decided I would just stick my head in the door and keep going. I figured I would start hanging back down at Bruce's. I needed to tighten my pool game back up because it had gotten a little rusty. When I walked into the pool room, it seemed as if everybody knew what my woman had done. There were sidebar conversations going on throughout the pool room while people were glancing over at me as if to say, "That's her man right there". Others would make little slick comments to get a rise out of me, which was common in the pool hall. I later decided to knock some balls around on a table by myself when someone came in and said, "Your woman's outside." I did not answer. I just kept knocking the balls around.

Finally, Cadillac Al walked in and said with a sarcastic grin on his face, "Your woman says for you to come outside for a minute. She wants to talk with you." I wasn't feeling it so I said, "Since you feel like you want to deliver messages tonight, you go back out there and tell her that I said that I ain't got no woman no more." She later tried again, sending Willie Harris, a friend who was always teaching me different moves with dice. Willie said, "Man, what's wrong with you? San is a good woman. Y'all ought to go somewhere and talk." All I could say was, "Naw, man, my rep is on the line. I can't do it." I continued to knock balls around.

Later, she called Nub Fingers at home to see if he could talk some sense into my head. Nub Fingers was like my street father. He had taught me much of what I knew about cards, women, and life. I spent more time with him than I had with my own biological father. I would travel with him to different pool halls while he wore white coveralls covered with paint, a white paint cap covered with paint, and a dried-up paintbrush in his hip pocket, pretending to be a painter who had just gotten paid. He would say he wanted to play a few games of pool for money if someone would consider giving him some odds since he was handicapped with no fingers on one of his hands. He was always quick to say that he had gotten them shot off in the war. Some sucker would always fall for it. Nub Fingers was one of the most notorious pool hustlers around. He was also a professional card shark. As he walked into the pool room, he grabbed me by my arm and marched me to a back table with everybody watching. "San asked me to talk to you. At least you could go out there and listen to what she has to say."

I said, "Yeah, but what are people gonna think?"

Nub shot back, "Damn what people think. Are they gone pay you like she's gonna pay you? And furthermore, she didn't have to do what she been doing for you. It just so happens that this woman really cares about you and what you think. The least you could do is go out there and listen to what she's got to say."

"Okay, I'll go out and listen to what she's got to say but my minds pretty much made up," I said.

When I stepped outside, she was standing there looking as if she had been crying. "Can we go somewhere and talk?" she asked.

I said, "No, we ain't going nowhere. Whatever you have to say, you can say it right here." Then she went on to explain that the papers were wrong. She had no intentions of testifying for the state. She only told them that she would when she was arrested a few months before on charges of prostitution just to get out of jail. However, last night, they had picked her up off the stroll and locked her up to make sure that she would appear to testify in court that morning. Even though they had picked her up the night before, she had no intentions of testifying, and they had postponed the case.

I told her that it would be best to go our separate ways. I didn't think that I could bear the shame of my woman being labeled a snitch. No matter what she said, I just couldn't seem to shake the shame of it all. She told me how wrong I was before walking into the night. Little did I know that it would be almost ten years before I would see her again. After San and I parted, I would hang around the pool halls with D.D. and a group of young hustlers my age and older, sharpening our skills in the various parlor games such as three-card monte, cards, pool, and dice. Every once and a while when money was too slow, I would have to do something radical like sell some dope or get with a crew that was breaking in a clothing store or some other kind of business.

I began carrying a crowbar in my belt and a screw-driver in my pocket, always ready to go at the drop of a hat. One night, we broke into a business and stole a large sum of money with a large checkbook containing the payroll checks. After dividing the money, no one wanted the hassle with the checkbook, except for me. The other guys were strictly cash-and-carry, but I knew that I could probably sell the whole book to a fence or get with a check-forging crew. I asked the guys to let me hold on to the checkbook to see what I could do with it. They were fine with that, saying, "Why don't you just go on and take them. We don't mess with no checks, no way. They're just too much of a hassle."

A couple of days later, I was running around with O.D. and Sorefeet. These two guys hustled pool, played petty con, and knew a whole lot about checks. They were masters of shady deals. You couldn't trust them as far as you could throw them. If nothing else, you could always count on them to put some dirt in the water. O.D. provided our transportation with an old '59 Cadillac along with a gift of gab and an ability to copy anybody's signature. Sorefeet provided all the IDs, and a lady teller who worked the drive-through window at one of the banks. Of course, she demanded her cut too. I provided the checks and kept a good eye on O.D. and Sorefeet. After having exhausted the poor woman in the drive-through teller window with checks from a hundred fifty to three hundred dollars throughout the morning, she got scared. She told us she wasn't going to take anymore checks and that she was afraid for her job. After that, they made a plan B.

This plan involved me taking all of the risks while they told me how much heart I had over the other guys my age. They pumped me up with how far I was going to go, how smart I was for my age, and all the stuff they were going to teach me. I went along, knowing that this was some game to keep me going. I started thinking that it was time for me to cut these guys loose. After cashing a couple of checks in the grocery store with a car full of groceries, I told them that it was time for me to go home because I had promised my mother that I would run a few errands for her before it got too late. Since they thought that I was young and naive, they trusted me to hold on to all the IDs and the remaining checks with the understanding that I would meet them the following day at Gibson's around twelve noon.

The next day, I was up bright and early. I was sitting in Bruce's Pool Room by eight looking to see who I would get to cash some checks with good ID because I had some fresh ID for an older man. In came Satchmo. We called him Satch, for short. He had just come out of the gambling joint next door to Bruce's, which was run by an old hustler named South Street. These smoke-filled gambling houses were all over town where gamblers would go from one joint to the next all night long. Satch came in Bruce's cussin' and fussin' that morning about how he just got broke and how much money he'd blown. He said he had been catching bad cards all night. Satch had been hanging between the pool halls and the gambling joints of Atlantic City for over forty years. He had the bio on every pimp, hustler, pool shark, and con man who ever came to town. Some nights when the action was slow, we'd all gather around while Satch would entertain us with the bios of this wonderful league of gentlemen. He was always quick to remind us that a good hustler should never get broke, that he should always leave himself something to hustle with, and always keep a one-way bus ticket in his wallet just in case you had to leave town in a hurry.

"Young Blood"—as he would call all of us young hustlers—"I been catchin' bad cards all week. Can't kill nothing and won't nothing die. Let me hold something before the girls get you. I can do better than that." So I went on to tell Satch about the checks I had and the ID to go along with them. Since I was providing everything that was needed, I would give him thirty dollars for each check that he would cash and all of the groceries that he would buy cashing them. I was surprised at how quick he jumped at the offer. I thought that he would at least haggle with me a bit and push me for a little more but he didn't. The first check that was cashed would be a dry run just to test the water. It worked like a charm. So for the rest of the morning, Satch and I were tied together at the hip, back and forth from the grocery store with arms full of groceries. We finished up about eleven thirty that morning, shaking hands for a job well done. This was the first time I had ever seen Satch smile since I had known him. He said, "You all right with me, Young Blood. You helped ol' Satch out today. If you ever need me again, you know where to find me." Satch left, walking up the street and looking as if he was going to jump and click his heels at any minute. I went shopping for a few new outfits and a pair of gators that I had my eyes on in one of the stores on the boardwalk.

I was supposed to meet up with O.D. and Sorefeet at noon but since I had no intention of doing that, I decided to stay off the set for a few days because I knew they would come looking for me. I figured this would be a good time to hook up with Racetrack. Racetrack turned me on to this drug called methedrine about a week before. Even though it had been a small amount, it kept me high for about nine hours. I liked it because it wasn't a downer like heroin. Plus, I could play pool with it. As a matter of fact, it seemed to enhance my game. It kept me calm. I could talk and read a book or two in one night, but the crash was awful. Racetrack had a friend in Philadelphia that sold this stuff in quantity. Nobody in Atlantic City was selling it so I convinced

Racetrack to take me to Philly so that I could buy enough to bring back to sell. A few days later, I was in business selling meth wrapped in little pieces of aluminum foil for five or ten dollars a crack with a personal stash of my own.

On the second night out, I was back in Bruce's playing six-ball for ten dollars a game. I was playing unusually good that night. It seemed that I could do no wrong. I was knocking the balls in the pockets as if they had radar. The meth that I snorted was working well with my game. As I finished my game, I looked to the front of the pool room and saw O.D. and Sorefeet standing by the register and watching me. They walked over and sat in a couple of chairs on the wall next to the table where I had been shooting. O.D started off, "Man, we need to talk."

"About what?" I said as if I didn't know.

Sorefeet then jumped in. "You know what you did. You crossed us."

I gave it right back and said, "Well, it ain't like y'all wasn't trying to cross me first. Call it what you want. I was just trying to protect my interest, and, furthermore, I felt you were already paid. Y'all know you wasn't doing me right, putting me out on Front Street and all."

After some going back and forth, I saw that I was going to have to give them something to get them off my back. I had a plastic bag full of meth wrapped in pieces of aluminum foil ready to be distributed. I asked them if they ever tried any meth before. "What's that?" O.D. asked.

I said, "This stuff can get you paid." I then took them into the restroom and let them snort some from the dollar bill containing my personal stash. After having taken a few snorts apiece, they nodded in approval. I gave them five pieces of foil-wrapped meth worth ten each. "Y'all take this and let bygones be bygones. I can't give you no money."

They said, "You know you wronged us, man. Where can we find you if we want some more later?"

"I'll be around, but you know you're going to have to cough up some bucks the next time." I would use meth for the next few months and chase it with a bag of heroin each night so that I wouldn't crash coming back down.

7

THE DOPE GORILLA

Later, I started selling dope for Smokey, the biggest and most notorious drug dealer in the town. Everybody knew Smokey and everybody knew that I had Smokey's dope. The Feds were always trying to catch Smokey but he would always manage to evade them. Once, two federal agents tried to arrest Smokey after having picked up his stash in an alley. Smokey whipped both the agents, ran, got rid of his dope, then came back to let them arrest him for assaulting two federal agents. He would don mink coats, mink hats, gold chains, and diamond rings and had multiple cars. To top it off, he worked as an electrician on the side.

I made more money at this point than I had ever seen and had a wardrobe to match. However, I began using more heroin than I had ever used. I went from snorting to skin-popping to mainlining the drug. By this time, Smokey hired another young kid to work with me by the name of Fatback. As both of our habits continued to escalate, we would help one another to re-up so that Smokey's money was straight. Before long, I had gotten to the point that I couldn't even help Fatback re-up for the monkey that was once on my back now turned into a full-grown gorilla. Smokey had to lift the package from me, saying, "Don't worry about the money you owe me, little bro. Just get yourself together." I was now strung out like a research monkey. Now I owed everybody, and they were all looking for me to hurt me. I was slipping in and out of doorways at night and hiding in the shadows, too ashamed to even show my face. It seemed as if I didn't have a friend in the world because I had turned them all into enemies.

I did have one friend left—my mom. So I decided I would pay her a visit. She was still living in public housing where I was raised. When she would see me, she would look me up and down and look at how my hair to determine if I needed a cut. Sometimes she would say, "They took too much off the top" or "I like it better when they give you a square" or some other comment concerning my hair. Then she would want to look at my eyes. She always knew when I was using. She would say, "Boy, you look a little peeked around the eyes. Are you catching a cold or something? Why don't you go in the room and get a little rest. You've been running too much. I'll wake you up a little later."

One time I went to visit. I went to take a nap. A couple of hours later, she woke me up saying that some friends of mine were waiting in the living room to see me. My first thought was, *How did anybody know that I'm here?* Maybe it was somebody with some dope they wanted me to try or someone looking for me to cop for them. As I entered the room, there standing in the middle of my mother's living room were two old junkies. I had shot dope with them several times. They were now preaching sobriety and peddling an outpatient program called New Well, which operated out of a storefront on Arctic Avenue. My mother had been talking to these guys about how to convince me that I needed some help. She seized the opportunity to call them while I was asleep. They told me I was killing my mother and I was going to send her to an early grave. She didn't deserve my carrying on the way I was. She worked hard to raise us and now she was worried that something would happen to me. She was worried that I would be killed or die from an overdose if I didn't get help while there was still time. I resented them talking to me like that while my mother cried and pleaded with me, saying, "They're only here to help you. Boy, you need some help."

Although they were right, I had a bad case of denial, pride, and stubbornness, and that three-fold defense is not easily broken. I cursed them for having the audacity to approach me like this and told them that they needed to leave because there was nothing wrong with me. It wasn't as bad as they were making it out to be. I felt that my mother betrayed me by calling them. My life became one long crime spree, trying to feed the dope gorilla that was now riding my back. I went in and out of jail for petty crimes ranging from shoplifting to breaking and entering. The heroin was so potent during that time that the turnkey in the jail would go around in the evening from cell to cell to see if anybody wanted to go to the hospital that evening to keep you from kicking the habit cold turkey. This was an offer that hardly anybody would refuse except for me.

My mother worked at the hospital as an Licensed Practical Nurse for many years and most of the doctors and nurses knew her. The last thing I wanted to do was to bring shame on her name so I would always refuse the hospital. I would try to kick cold turkey, not wanting to bring any more shame on my mother than I already had. Once I was released, I would continue in my crime spree. It seemed like every cop and citizen in the world was looking to catch me. The only place I could take refuge would be at mom's house. She would try and convince me how much I needed help, that I wasn't looking like myself or dressing like I once did. I lost a considerable amount of weight, my hair needed cutting, and my shoes were ragged. "Reggie, let me take you to the New Well", she pleaded. "I've already paid the twelve-dollar entry fee for you to get in. Since I gave them my last money, you should at least try, boy."

I reluctantly agreed to go and just as reluctantly followed behind her to the little storefront program. It was the first one of its kind to attempt to address the escalating problem of heroin addiction in Atlantic City. It would later become an institution called Narco. Today, it is known as John Brooks Recovery Center. There was no such thing as Narcotics Anonymous in those days. This was the era of the "up in your face" therapeutic meetings. The older guys would try to encourage me by telling me that if I would get it together, a lot of other younger guys would come in too. I really didn't want to be in those meetings. Since Mom paid, I had a few court cases, and a number of people were looking for me, I could not come up with a good reason to not be there...yet.

By this time, as my mother would say, I had every kind of case except for a suitcase. This was the one time I was ready to go wherever the judge would send me and serve whatever sentence he was ready to give me because I had made such a mess of my life. If I continued at the pace I was going, I would surely be dead before long. I was eventually picked up on a parole violation and sitting on a pile of cases. The prosecutor told my attorney that if I would take a guilty plea, they would bring all of the charges together, offering me a five-year indeterminate sentence. I took it. Otherwise, I would have been facing at least thirty years.

8

YARDVILLE

I was sentenced to do my time in an institution called Yardville. My job there was in the kitchen on the serving line. One day, I came into the dining hall early to shoot the breeze with some friends that were locking on another unit. In the corner was a group of guys playing dice. The shooter was a tall, light-skinned brother with curly hair. Everybody called him Whitefolks. He was about my age, serving ten years for shooting and killing a fellow in a dice game for trying to take his money back. As I approached, I noticed that the dice were hand-carved soap. Whitefolks had been winning the entire commissary as he switched in and out with another pair of dice undetected. I began to place my bets on him until the game was broken up by an officer. Whitefolks and I became best friends since we had so much in common, having both come up in the pool halls very young. We both learned the safely guarded secrets of cheating in dice and cards at an early age. For the next year or so, several of us would come together almost daily to sharpen our skills in cards and dice in preparation for the streets. Others would spend their time lifting weights, playing basketball, boxing, singing, and playing dominoes or checkers. The only thing

I did with the other guys was play chess and I became very good at it.

Every now and then, an Atlantic City newspaper would find its way to one of the homeboys and would be passed around to keep us abreast of what was happening back home. One morning, I came into the chow hall, went through the serving line, and took my seat to eat when I noticed that none of my homeys were talking. Everybody seemed unusually quiet. "What's the matter with y'all this morning? Somebody die?"

"Naw, Reg, we just got done reading the paper. They got your name in here for sale and possession of narcotics."

I said, "Now how can that be? I'm already serving a five-year indeterminate sentence!"

At that point, a short kid named Spider lifted the paper from the table with both hands and handed it to me. "Here, man, read it for yourself." Spider was paralyzed in both hands after having shot some bad dope one night. He could no longer use his hands or fingers. It seemed that all the muscles had collapsed in both hands.

The paper went on to say that there was a large drug bust in Atlantic City and listed all of the names of the people that had been arrested. Among those names, to my surprise, was my own! My first thought was, *How can this be? I'm already incarcerated!* Then I thought, *How could somebody be stupid enough to use my name, as bad as my name was already?* A few days later, I received a piece of mail regarding a secret indictment for sales and possession of narcotics. I was to appear in court within the next month. The day of my court appearance, I was taken to Mays Landing for my first hearing along with a white guy who owned a nightclub in Atlantic City. As we rode to court that morning, I asked him why he was going to court since he too had already gotten his time. "Man, I don't know why they dragging me down here this morning. Ain't nobody trying to tell me nothing."

Later after having sat in a cell for most of the morning, my attorney pulled me into a room and said "They got you for a sale you made before you were sentenced to the time you're serving now. What's more, the guy you came in the van with this morning is the guy who turned state's evidence on you. He is going to testify that you sold him some drugs, and there was an agent present to witness the sale going down. I'm afraid you ain't got no win. At best, you can take a guilty plea to a lesser charge. I think that I can get the sale knocked off and you just plea to a possession, which only carries five years."

I needed some time to think so I entered a "not guilty" plea and awaited trial, which would be several months down the road. In the meantime, I would get in this guy's head to see why he would even try to turn state evidence on me since he had to come back to Yardville to live. Once word got back that he was a snitch and was going to turn state on me, there was no way that he could live in the general population without his life being in danger. This was not an atmosphere that took kindly to snitches and child molesters. They always lived in the shadow of death and in constant fear of their lives.

When it was time to go back to the institution, it would be just me along with two armed guards, while the other guy would be shipped to another institution for safekeeping. About a year later, I was released to the Mays Landing county jail to await sentencing for the secret indictment. I decided not to go to trial and take a guilty plea for possession of narcotics instead of the sale. I threw myself at the mercy of the court. Since I had already served time and was paroled to the county, I thought that the judge would have mercy and run whatever sentence he would give me together with the old. That would put me back on the streets. Once the judge glanced over my record, he decided that he'd give me another five years running wild. In other words, it was to be started immediately as if I had never served a day. I was handcuffed and shackled to return to Yardville, which also acted as a reception institution where everyone sentenced in Jersey had to pass through before being shipped to the institution where they would serve their time. From Yardville, I was shipped to a rougher institution called Bordentown that housed about six hundred young men.

After arriving at Bordentown, I was sent to B wing, which had three tiers. I was locked on B-2, which seemed to house most of the guys that were in for armed robbery from throughout Jersey. Most of the guys from North Jersey robbed banks but were too young to go to the federal penitentiary, so they would serve their sentences in Bordentown. These guys were unrepentant bank robbers, sitting around and boasting about how many banks they had robbed and how much money they had gotten. They would sit around demonstrating the various methods they had used in robbing banks such as how to jump up on the bank counter, the best way to hold the pistol, what they would say to the tellers, and how to instill the greatest fear. This was crazy! At the same time, it was fascinating to see so many young guys my age who carried pistols, robbed banks, and were passionate enough about robbing banks to practice how they would be doing it again. Every day they would run up and down the tier, sliding cell doors open and shouting "Freeze! This is a stick up!" Although it was interesting to watch, it never piqued my interest enough to want to become a bank robber myself.

I went back to sharpening my skills with cards and dice and enjoying everybody's commissary as I would beat them at blackjack, tonk, and poker at the card table, even the young bank robbers. Hardly anybody knew the depth of my knowledge when it came to the various ways of cheating at cards, except for a few homeboys, and I would share my winnings with them. One day, while putting my winnings in a box underneath my bunk, my cell door suddenly slid open. When I looked up, there was this wild kid everybody called Carrot Top standing in the door. Rumor had it that he had raped a woman repeatedly, told her that he would be back seven the next night, and that she had better not tell anybody. Needless to say, the police were there waiting to arrest this kook when he returned.

As Carrot Top stepped all the way in my cell, another inmate slid the cell door behind him, saying, "Longcrier, everybody's been saying you've been cheating us with them cards."

"Oh yeah?" I said as I stalled for time, trying to figure out my next move. One of us was going to draw a bad decision out of this situation, and I wasn't planning on it being me. I said, "Man, if you think I was cheating, show me what you think I did to you."

He wasn't stopping. "Shut up. I don't want to hear that slick stuff out of you."

I said, "Okay, man, I just don't want no trouble. I'm just trying to do my time and get out of here." I reached under my bunk and passed him a small box that contained some nabs and a couple candy bars.

I watched the muscles in his face suddenly relax. "Yeah, that's what I'm talking about."

I said, "Man, I just don't want no trouble. I'm trying to get out of here on a post-conviction release. Let me give you the key to my locker. Y'all can have all this stuff. It just ain't worth the trouble."

I reached into my pillow to grab hold of a trusty weapon from the early days of the reformatory, the old reliable lock in the sock. I made it a point to keep one in my pillow in every institution for occasions like this one. I continued to talk to Carrot Top about how I always respected him, and that I just wanted to get along. All the while, I was making sure that I had a good grip on the sock containing the lock and gradually easing it from the inside of the pillow with cold and lethal calculation. I knew I had to make the first shot count or else I would be done. As I slowly stood up, I said, "Here, man, take this key." I swung with the first blow crashing across the bridge of his nose. When I saw the blood gush out, he grabbed his nose saying, "You mf, you busted my nose!" I knew then that I was home free and began to make quick work out of Carrot Top with my lock in a sock. He was hollering for someone to help him while trying to get out of my cell. I refused to let him out and I was not willing to let anybody else in until I was sure that I wouldn't have Carrot Top or any of his homeboys coming back on me ever again. My intent was to instill fear in him that would make him think twice before approaching me again.

By the time the tier officer came, Carrot Top was lying on the floor of my cell in a puddle of his own blood. "What's going on here, Longcrier?"

I said, "This man tried to come in my cell and take my stuff, sir. Plus, he said he was going to rape me like he did that woman on the street, sir." I was making it seem worse than it really was.

Once he saw that it was Carrot Top, he said, "Carrot Top, I told you somebody was going to hurt you one day. You got just what you deserved. Longcrier, get a mop and bucket and clean this mess up. I'm not going to write you up because he ain't had no business coming in your cell in the first place and he had it coming to him. This punk has been running around here taking stuff and getting away with it. Longcrier, don't you think you got away with nothing because if you did this to anybody else, I'd lock your black behind up. Now gather your bunk and junk because you're going upstairs to B-3."

9

BACK ON THE STREETS

Within the next six months, I was on my way back to court on a post-conviction relief, which my attorney had filed after I had been sentenced. This was a legality that was usually granted to a defendant for excessive sentencing. My attorney felt that I was a good candidate. I had a good chance to get some granted since I had been given this sentence on top of the five-year indeterminate sentence I finished serving, never having even hit the streets. Once I got back in front of the judge with an attorney pleading my case, he asked the judge to run my sentences together, giving me credit for the time I served in the county so that I could go home. The judge was merciful this time and granted my release.

Once out, I was glad to be home. I headed straight to the refrigerator to see what I could find to eat. Although I was glad to see my mother and she was glad to see me, I didn't have time to stick around because the streets were calling me once again. I had people I needed to see and places I needed to go. I kissed my mother on the cheek and told her I had to go. As I headed toward the door, she gently grabbed my arm, saying, "Son, can you talk to your mother for just a minute?

Just sit down and talk to me just a little bit. You are my son and you know I care about you, don't you?" I said, "Yeah, Mom, but what is it? I've got to go." "Reggie, can I ask you a question? After all, I'm your mother and your mother ought to have the right to ask you a question." I said, "Okay, Mom. What is it? I got to go!" She was firm with me, "Now, boy, you been in all these jails and served all this time. You just got out and you're ready to run right back to them same streets, to those same friends that got you in trouble in the first place. You can't even spend five minutes with your mother? Are you crazy? Have you lost your mind in that place? You can tell me, I'm your mother. I can make some calls and get you some help. I think you need to see a psychiatrist." All I could say was, "Aw, Mom! I'm going." As I headed out the door, I added, "See you later."

It was customary for hustlers who got out of jail or prison to make their rounds in the pool halls, skin joints, bars, and gambling houses throughout the city. People were always there who were glad to see you home. They would tell you how good you looked and give you some money to help you get on your feet as a homecoming gift. The second day I was out, D.D., my old partner, came into the pool hall. Happy to see me, he rushed over and hugged me as we customarily did when welcoming someone just fresh from the joint. He reached in his pocket, handed me a roll of twenty-dollar bills, and said, "I'm glad you home, man. Come on outside with me. I've got something to show you." As I walked outside with D.D., in front of the poolroom was a brand-new Cyclone Spoiler. "How you like it, Reg?" he said.

I was amazed. "Is that yours?"

"Yeah!" he exclaimed.

"Get in, let me take you for a spin"

I took slid on the passenger side, surveying the interior and all of the different gadgets. I looked at D.D. in amazement. "Can you really drive this car, man?" I asked. "When I left the streets, I remember you couldn't drive." Then I went through a battery of questions I needed him to answer before I would let him drive off. "How long you been driving? Who taught you how to drive? Let me see your driver's license and registration." It was hard for me to believe that D.D. was driving legally. I remembered the last time D.D. pulled up to the pool hall to get me. This was years before when we were in our young teens and he had stolen a car to go joyriding. We didn't get two blocks before he had wrecked the car, hitting three or four cars in the process. We both jumped out and ran through alleys and over fences, trying to avoid the police.

Now D.D. was behind the wheel again, but this time, claiming to be a good driver with his own car, a valid license, and registration to match. Reluctantly, I directed him to drive slow. He pulled out of the parking space slowly and headed uptown. After having gone through several lights and turning some corners, I was finally convinced that D.D. really could drive. When we drove back up in front of the pool hall, D.D. popped the trunk of his car. He said he had something else to give me that would help get me back on my feet. He reached in his trunk and handed me about twelve brand-new watches still in the box with $250 price stickers and about five rings sparkling from little boxes with a velvety backdrop. "Man, this is better than the slum we used to sell from New York years ago," I said.

He explained, "While you were gone, I found a couple of new slum shops over in Philly. Plus, they are a dollar or two cheaper."

Slum was a term used for fake or counterfeit jewelry. The watches would be name brand such as Seiko, Longines, Omega, and Rolex. They were fake, one-jewel watches that could be purchased for no more than five bucks apiece with the box, stickers and all. If you sneezed on them, they would stop running. The rings that appeared to be diamonds were cut glass that would make a diamond cry. These little slum shops were not known or open to the public. They always gave the appearance of being closed. If one was open to the public, they would sell things other than jewelry. You couldn't buy this kind of jewelry unless you were known or someone brought you in by the hand and introduced you as another slum hustler. This was another of the many hustles we had on the trail to get rich quick. This was just the boost I needed to get back on my feet. I would sell this slum in no time. I asked D.D. to drop me at the house to unload this stuff, and pick me up in the morning so we could get busy.

The next morning D.D. was at my mother's house picking me up. Within hours, we sold most of the slum we had. By two that afternoon, we were headed for Philly to reload. As we entered the little shop on Market Street, a little bald-headed white man with wire-rimmed glasses looked up from tinkering with a watch. Seeing D.D, he asked, "You got rid of that last load already?"

"Yeah, man. This is my partner. I told you he was getting out."

The man looked me up and down. "So you the Reggie that D.D.'s been telling me so much about?"

D.D. chimed in, "He's a better slum hustler than I am when he's up on his game."

After the small talk, the little man walked us over to a display case in the back of the store in a corner. "This is some of the best stuff I've got" he said as he showed us a wide range of watches, gold chains, and rings. After spending more than an hour and a half putting our watches and rings in their individual boxes with stickers and price tags, we headed back to Atlantic City. We decided we would go home, change, and then come back out to work the bars and clubs. Afterward, we would look for some action in the pool halls. For the next couple of days, D.D. and I were hustling nonstop to see who could outsell the other. That Sunday, we rested in the pool hall, sitting around and shooting the breeze.

In the meantime, a tall, dark-skinned prostitute named Carol walked in. I had known Carol for years. She and San (my ex) were tight and took a lot of money from tricks together. Carol was what they called a renegade because she chose not to have a man that she would have to pay to protect her from being prey to the dangerous elements in the streets. She rushed over to me and kissed me on the cheek. "Hi, baby, I heard you were home." She reached in her bra and handed me some money. "This is a little something to help you get on your feet. I know everybody else gave you something but I just wanted to give you a little something. You know we cool."

"Is this an indication of things to come?" I said jokingly. "Does this mean you ready to choose a man?"

She smiled and then said, "Maybe." I went on to press her to take a chance on me. Then she told me how she was skeptical, fearing I would get back on that heroin. She said it had turned me into a monster before I left. I had not been myself and I wasn't on top of my game. I told her that was behind me now and that I was road ready. She said, "We'll see." It gave me a glimmer of hope.

The next morning, I was sitting up in the bed contemplating my day when I sensed someone standing in the doorway of my bedroom. As I looked up, D.D was standing there grinning. "Your mom told me I could come up and see if you were awake yet." D.D. was the only one of my friends she would trust to come up to my room like that.

"What's up?" I asked. "It's seven o'clock in the morning. What you doing out so early?"

He told me about how he and Little George was gambling, and playing pool the night before after I went home. Little George flipped on him and tricked him into a dice game but George's game was far superior to his. George was one of the skilled gamblers who had many ways to cheat you in dice or cards. If I hung around any longer the night before, I would have saved D.D. from the trouble of George breaking him. Now it was done. It was what it was. As a result, D.D. went on a rampage, robbing gas stations and stores to replenish the stash he lost the night before. By the time he reached my house, he was pulling out money from all pockets. He told tell me how sweet this money was and that he had been robbing different places for over a year now. He said he was the ski-mask bandit who had eluded the police all this time! After he had counted the larger bills on my bed, he handed me all the ones and fives, which amounted to a little over four hundred dollars. He said he was on his way to rob another place that morning. It was a number drop and he was going to rob it before they could take the money to the bank that morning. A fence gave him this information in confidence, expecting to get a split of the take once it was done. D.D. said if I went with him to pull it off, we'd leave the fence out and split the money down the middle. The take would be anywhere from six to ten grand.

"Man, I'm a lot of things but I'm not a stick-up kid. Man, they're giving cats twenty years for that kind of stuff, and I ain't been on the streets a good six days yet. Man, it's kind of hard to believe that you the one that the papers been calling the ski-mask bandit, running around here with a pistol and a ski mask and sticking these places up." D.D. said, "Then how you think I got this car then? I didn't get the car I'm driving selling no slum. Look, man, I just wanted to put you down because you are my friend, but if you don't want to be down, I can understand. I'll just do it by myself." He then turned around and headed back down the stairs. Before he would get to the bottom of the steps, I called him back. I had become suddenly overwhelmed with larceny, greed, and a teaspoon of jealousy. I couldn't stand to think that D.D. was going to have so much more money than I had, especially if he pulled this job off by himself. Plus, he already had a new car and I was walking. I had a long way to catch up since I had only been out of prison less than a week. "D.D., hold up! Let me get washed up and dressed. I think I'll go with you."

Suddenly a big grin came across his face. "Man, I'm glad you changed your mind because I brought this gun just for you." He pulled out a brand-new German Luger from a bag along with a ski mask. Showing me his ski mask covered with dollar signs, he beamed with pride as he said, "This is the one I always wear."

By nine thirty that morning, I found myself walking into the Cardiff Liquor Store on Cardiff Circle. Following behind D.D. with pistols drawn, I told the man behind the counter, "This is a stickup, don't make it a homicide!"

D.D. ushered the man to a back office where the safe was located and told the man to open the safe. The man was so frightened that he momentarily forgot the combination. D.D. told him what he would do to him if he didn't open the safe. If he wanted to see his family again, he'd better do the right thing. As the man struggled to remember, he said, "Sixty, sixty, sixty." The safe finally opened. In the meantime, a couple of customers were in the front of the store, calling for someone to wait on them. We snatched money and bank bags and rushed back to the front. We passed the customers, went out the front door, and got into the car where everyone could see as we pulled off. We headed back to Atlantic City with D.D. driving and me down in the back seat trying to get a count of the take.

As we were driving over the Albany Avenue Bridge, D.D. said that a police car had just gotten behind him. We weren't sure he was after us so I told D.D. to cut a couple corners to see if he would stay behind us. We turned several corners once we were over the bridge and the cruiser stayed behind us. D.D. said we were going to have to make a fast break. The next thing I knew, we were in a high-speed chase with police cars and sirens in pursuit of us. I crouched down in the back seat. Looking up occasionally, I asked D.D., "Are we going to make it?"

With serious concentration on his face, he'd say, "If I get to the expressway, I believe I can lose 'em." I looked up as we were going through the expressway toll and the speedometer read 120. I laid back down in the back seat.

After about what seemed to be hours, no one appeared to be chasing us anymore. As we were approaching Toms River on the parkway, it seemed that we were the only one there with the exception of a car farther behind us. It seemed that we had shaken the police and we were home free. I breathed a sigh of relief and started congratulating D.D. and praising him for his good driving. "Yeah, man, but you ain't going to believe this. We just ran out of gas!" he said as he pulled the car off the parkway. The lone car that had been behind us was a highway patrol car that was told to follow us at a distance. A roadblock was ahead of us with state troopers and sheriffs waiting to give us a warm welcome if we had made it that far. The trooper pulled up behind us, drew his pistol, and motioned for us to throw out our weapons, get out of the car, and spread-eagle on the highway.

10

TRENTON STATE PRISON

After spending about six months in Mays Landing, I pleaded guilty to robbery and was sentenced to serve four to six years in Trenton State Prison. I got a five-year indeterminate sentence in the institution I had just left and only did about fifteen months. Now I would have to serve at least four years and nine months in the state prison.

The Trenton State Prison was a gruesome, Gothic-looking edifice with high walls that was built in 1849. That's a hundred years before I was born. This prison had been built smack-dab in the middle of the state of New Jersey's capital city, Trenton. What a place to put a prison! As we entered the entrance gate, I couldn't help but think about all the stuff that I had done that led me to such a horrible fate. I was so young. I had just turned twenty-one while in the county waiting to be sentenced. Now I was in this medieval-like confinement. The danger was so thick you could cut it with a knife. A big, burly guard began to bark orders. Everybody had to strip down naked and stand facing him. "Lift your sacks," he said, pointing to our privates. "Now turn around, bend over, and spread 'em. Raise your right foot, soles facing me. Left foot, turn back around. Now head for the showers." Everyone was handed a metal wash bucket, a bar of green lye soap, a wash cloth, a towel, a toothbrush, and a toothpaste. Then we were handed a white smock-like uniform top and bottoms that were like pajamas and some shower shoes. We were given a number in exchange for our names. Mine was 50378. All the new inmates entering Trenton were to wear these whites to distinguish them from the rest of the prison population. We were called "new fish." Another distinguishing mark was that all the new inmates in those days would have their heads shaved bald.

We were led to the cell block called reception or quarantine that held the new inmates. We had to pass through a place called the center, which was a large barren area right in the middle of the prison. It contained five iron gates that lead to the seven wings of the prison. All prison traffic had to pass through this circular area. Some people would refer to it as "the Star" because in the center of the floor was a star where guards would stand as cops directed the traffic in the institution with a blackjack in hand. "All right, seven wing coming out! Move it out seven wing! Hold it over there two wing! No talking! If I have to tell y'all one more time, you bastards will go last," they would say while directing traffic. "All right, four wing, move it out, hands out your pockets, shirt tails in, no horseplay!" This would go on throughout the day. Sometimes during the inmate movements, the prison band would play while the various wings would pass through the center on their way to the yard.

We were all directed to one wing where new inmates were housed before being let out into the general population. I was to lock in a three-tier cell for the next twenty-eight to thirty days. When we arrived, it was just about chow time and they would always feed the new fish with the gangsters from the various crime families and those who had special diets. After about a month or so in quarantine, I was sent to seven wing where the cells were arranged on tiers—seven right, seven left, and seven up. I was to lock on seven up. I learned that I probably wouldn't be in Trenton long before they would ship me out to another prison called Leesburg. Trenton kept most of the longtimers, lifers, and most dangerous criminals in the state. Working was a privilege, otherwise you were locked down about eighteen hours a day with the exception of yard and chow.

The dining hall was a death trap because that was where most of the stabbings would take place. For that reason, you would eat your food quickly and get out of there. A tall young fellow was there called Money. He was a few years older than me. He was serving twelve years. He and I would always walk to the chow hall or yard together. Money was locked in a cell on the tier above mine so we would wait on each other to go to chow every day even though we sat at different tables. I would sit with my homeboys from Atlantic City while Money would sit with his homeboys from Newark. That's the way it was. Most hometowns had certain tables where they would sit and no one else would sit there unless invited. The Muslims, the mafia, and the sissies had their own tables.

One day as I stood at the bottom tier waiting for Money to come down for chow, he suddenly appeared with a grim and troubled look on his face. "What's the matter, man?" I asked. He put his hand on my shoulder, saying, "Little bro,"—as he called me because he was a little older and much taller—"you just go on in ahead of me today because you don't want to be a part of what I'm getting ready to do." "What happened?" I asked. He answered, "That punk *white hat* disrespected me on the yard today in front of some people, showing off. I'm going to show him who he's messing with. I'm killing him today. Today he's going to die at my hands." The lieutenants and sergeants were all called "white hats" by the inmates because of their status. However, it was hard to believe that

65

he would want to kill this particular white hat because most of the inmates got along with this guy and liked him. Plus, he wasn't known as a show-off and didn't give the inmates a hard time. I couldn't really understand Money's reasoning, but then in matters like that in the penitentiary, you just had to mind your business and watch your own back. I went on ahead of Money as he had asked me.

As I entered the chow hall, this particular white hat and two others were moving the crowd of inmates as they entered. Seconds after passing by him, I heard a loud thump. When I turned around to see what was going on, Money was on the back of this white hat with one arm wrapped around his neck and the free hand repeatedly striking death blows to his neck, head, and shoulders with a shiv (prison knife). He fell to the floor with Money still on his back continuing to stab him as if he wanted to make sure that he'd never get up again. Other inmates were passing by coming in or out of the dining hall as if nothing was happening while several guards struggled to get Money off of their fallen comrade. It was too late, the damage had been done. This would be the first of many stabbings that I would witness while in prison over the years.

This prison had such a charged, volatile atmosphere that you would have to psych yourself up to instantly change in the phone booth of your mind into a killer if necessary in order to survive. The prison yard was another death trap, which the inmates called the "big dusty." It was a big field of hard-packed dirt with no sign of flowers, grass, or life. It was washed down in oil every day to keep the soil from blowing away. The big dusty was surrounded by four walls and covered by four gun towers with ready shooters waiting to blow your brains out at the slightest hint of disorder. At one wall were the handball courts. Chess, checkers, and dominos were played at another wall. The weight lifters were in one corner of the yard, boxers in the opposite corner, and a ball field in the middle. About thirty black militants ran around the yard every day wearing black T-shirts and red bandanas. One was falling behind, trying to keep up. Along the walls, various groups came together according to their professions. We had pimps driving imaginary Cadillacs around the yard and bragging about what they had and how many women they had pimped. Stickup boys would talk about the jobs they had pulled off. Moving down the wall were con men, number backers, gamblers, racketeers, counterfeiters, dope boys, and homeboys. This was a breeding ground for any type of criminal you wanted to be. In one corner, you could see the sissies picking pimples off the faces of their lovers. Two things that would be quickly killed over in prison were sissies and money.

Soon after I arrived at the prison, there was a sissy named Poochie who was a homey always looking out for the Atlantic City boys coming in. This was tradition among homeboys to make sure you had some commissary until you were able to get on your feet. One day, Poochie brought me a bag with some cosmetics, deodorant, soap, and a few cakes and candy bars. "Here, Reg, I gathered these things for you to hold you over." I took the bag and thanked Poochie for the stuff. We had been friends since I had protected him from a trick that was trying to kill him on the streets for rolling him.

Once I had taken the bag, Big Hawk, who was sitting in front of me said, "Reg, don't turn around now but three tables behind us, his man is watching. You better watch out. He may think you're some joker that wants his sissy."

I quickly called Poochie back, "Make sure you tell your man that I'm just your homeboy. You go and tell him right now before he starts some mess." I didn't want to turn around. I just told Hawk to watch and make sure he did.

As Poochie went to tell his man that I was just his homeboy, Hawk watched closely. He saw Poochie's man nod okay while Poochie explained the situation then tapped him twice on his behind, sending him away. Hawk said "Okay, you can relax. It's cool." Hawk knew Poochie's man for years and had watched him cut up several guys over his sissy, sometimes just for staring too long. Hawk was watching my back, and I really appreciated it. I found out that Poochie's man was doing a life sentence for murder and didn't mind committing murder again, especially when it came to his sissy.

The prison movie hall was just above the inmate dining hall. The steps leading up to the movie hall was another one of the many death traps. It wasn't unusual to be on the way up or down while stepping over or around an inmate who had been stabbed multiple times by an assailant trying to slip away into the moving traffic. During weekdays, the movie hall would become the TV room. Each wing would have the privilege to watch TV one night a week for about an hour on one of the TVs that sat in one of the four corners of the room. Other inmates would play chess, checkers, cards, or some other board game to pass the time.

My job assignment was to make New Jersey license plates in the prison tag shop. I was so tired of hanging tags every day until one morning, I came into the shop and hid behind a box of tags and went to sleep. It wasn't long before the head man over the shop discovered my hiding place and was waking me up, saying "Longcrier, I believe you're a little too expensive for me. Why don't I just send you back to your wing so that you can finish sleeping in your cell?"

11

LEESBURG PRISON

They never called me back to work, and no one said anything to me until months later when they were calling me to ship out to another prison in the southern part of Leesburg. My job assignment now would be to work in the state tailor shop, laying out material and cutting the patterns for the prison uniforms. Leesburg had only been open a year, and the units that held inmates were not all open yet.

While established prison hustles were yet to be born in such a new prison, an older homey of mine, So, decided that we would partner and monopolize the pie business. So So was a slick-talking intellectual who always carried a book and had command of the English language like no one I had ever seen. He could be very arrogant and a force to reckon with so most of the inmates would rather get their pies from me. Eventually, I had to cut So So loose because his out-of-control temper and arrogance would end up putting us out of business. We decided to split the business and go our separate ways. He took the right side of the walkway leading to the upstairs dining hall, and I took to the left side. He cussed me out and called me every kind of a name except for a child of God. I felt a little bad for cutting him loose because he contributed to a proposal that I had given the warden for a drug program in B unit where I was locking. It was called Alpha Meta, which meant the beginning of a change.

After working in the tailor shop for several months, I requested to change jobs to the downstairs kitchen with the officer's dining room. This was supposed to be a sweet job. The food served to the officers was better than the food served to the inmates. There was one hitch, all of the new inmates that came in to work at the downstairs kitchen had to start out first washing pots and pans before he could move on to an assigned job. When I came in, I took the place of another guy who was working there for a couple of weeks and was allowed to go on to his assigned job. I worked with another inmate by the name of Butch. Weeks later, another inmate came in to take Butch's place so that he could go to his assigned job. Next to handling the garbage detail, this was the dirtiest and most thankless job in the prison. You would have to wash big, tall pots and pans all day long over a large sink after each meal. It would be a month before another inmate came who was newer than I was. He was an older convict who was known to the guards and kitchen supervisor. He had a little clout. This guy was privileged to come in and bypass the pots and pans, going straight to his assigned job without relieving me on the pots and pans.

My first reaction to this was to quit. I wanted to just walk out and deal with the consequences later. Two older convicts who were cooks observed what was going down and came over to caution me about the consequences. They said I shouldn't do something that I would regret later without talking to the kitchen supervisor first. I took their advice. I went to the supervisor and explained the problem I was having with not being transferred to another job assignment since a new man came into the kitchen. He just looked at me as if I was plumb out of my mind and shrugged me off as if it didn't matter. He said, "Get back to them pots and pans before I write your stupid behind up!"

I wanted to quit then but I had one more card to play, the warden. He would come into the officer's dining hall at about ten most mornings to have his coffee. I figured he'd have a sympathetic ear once I reminded him that I was the inmate who put the proposal together for the drug program in B unit. I was shocked to find out that it didn't matter much to him either. All he wanted to do was finish drinking his coffee and be left alone. I had just about had it. I quit, leaving one lone pot washer and piles of pots and pans. As I walked back to my unit, I heard some footsteps coming from behind. I turned around to see Casey, the lone dishwasher trying to catch up with me. He said that he just couldn't stay there by himself to wash all of them pots and pans. By the time I reached my unit, the kitchen supervisor was calling the unit officer and telling him to send me back to the kitchen. If we were not back there in five minutes, he was going to write us up and make sure we go to the hole for ten days. The hole was another jail inside the jail that was segregated from the rest of the population. Its cells were small with wooden slabs attached to the walls where you slept on with no mattress and pillow. The cells were called French cells because the toilets were nothing but a round hole on the floor of the cell with a button in the wall to flush it.

That evening, Casey and I appeared before the disciplinary committee called the court line to answer to the write-ups. Our fate would be decided here. A long line was present that evening, waiting to see this committee for various crimes committed in the penitentiary. They had write-ups for things ranging from possession of contraband to attempted murder. Casey and I were in the back of the line. Finally, they called Casey's name first. As soon as he came back out,

I asked what happened. He said they said that they would give him a chance to go back to the kitchen and finish the pots and pans. If he did, they would drop the write-up. If he didn't go back, they'd give him ten days in the hole. He decided he would go back to the kitchen and finish washing the pots and pans. Soon, they were calling for me. I went in and pleaded my case as best I could but it seemed to fall on deaf ears. They said they would make the same offer to me that they made to Casey, go back and finish washing those pots and pans or do ten days in the hole. By this time, I was furious because nobody seemed to understand how unfair they had been to me. Their only concern was getting those pots and pans washed.

I said, "How about y'all finishing them pots and pans yourselves since you're that concerned about them being washed. I'll just take the ten days in the hole. To me, it's just another place in the same prison." From the looks on their faces, they were obviously not prepared for my response. Since the hole was full and had a waiting list, I was put on LIS (lock in status). That meant that I would be confined to my cell on the unit twenty-four hours a day with my meals being brought to my cell, losing all privileges until a cell in the hole came open for me to serve my ten days.

About five days later after having finished my breakfast tray, I heard the sound of leg chains, shackles, and handcuffs. "Longcrier! Get your bunk and junk."

"What is it this morning, the hole?" I asked.

"I'm afraid not, son," said one of the officers looking at the papers in his hand. "We have orders to ship you back to Trenton this morning behind the Walls."

"Wait a minute! You sure you got that right? I'm supposed to be waiting to go to the hole," I said.

"I'm sorry, son, but our orders are to take you back to maximum security. Step out of the cell."

As I stepped out, they put the leg irons around my ankles and chain across my waist then cuffed my hands. I was led out of the unit that morning flanked by two guards with one on each side. As I looked ahead, there was So So perched on the wall leading to the chow hall. As we passed him, he was nodding, saying, "See there, boy. God don't like ugly." He was suggesting that with me gone, he'd have the pie business all to himself.

12

BACK TO TRENTON STATE PRISON

When I arrived back behind the wall of Trenton State Prison, it was the same old chaos, violence, and turmoil. All the while, the prison band played on. This time, I would lock in a cell on 2 Left. I didn't know anybody on 2 wing, with the exception of a couple of homeboys that locked on the other side on 2 right, which housed all of the inmates that worked in the kitchen. The only time I'd see most of my homeys would be during yard or chow. It was possible to go for months in prison without seeing anybody you knew if they were on another wing.

Most of my time on the yard were spent hanging with con men, card sharks, and pimps who would always try to stay clear of the violence and chaos that made up the prison atmosphere. Although these guys were from various parts of the country, they landed together by a spirit of allegiance and love for the game. This was a tight-knit circle that was not easily infiltrated. Most times, they stayed to themselves on the yard because there were tricks, schemes, and strategies that were safely guarded amongst this group as if they were military secrets.

One of the friendships that developed from this group of hustlers was with another younger fellow named Gene who was from Washington. He was in for bank robbery. Although he was a few years older than me, we were the youngest of the group. Gene and I would study and rehearse lines from a manuscript that was passed around called *The Modern Players*. It had been written by an old-timer in the prison and was only to be shared with a chosen few.

As the months passed, a list of characters came to the prison from home. In some way or another, their lives were strongly tied to mine. Some were friends; some were foes. Sammy was an enemy when I left the street. We had gotten in an argument in the pool hall over some money and it ended in a fistfight behind the pool room. He came to prison over another pool hall fight. This time, he shot the guy he was fighting with. Sammy was a tall, good-looking guy with nice hair who still had his baby skin. Convicts would gather to see him as if he were a female.. As he walked into the chow hall, inmates would taunt him, blow kisses, tell him how fine he was, and ask him if there was anything he needed. I could see from the expression on his face he was apprehensive and afraid. I watched him scan the dining hall for a safe place to sit, and he saw me for the first time sitting at the table closest to the dish room. This was the Atlantic City section where we would sit every day for every meal. A glimmer of hope came across his face and then vanished just as quickly. I knew he was wondering whether or not we were still enemies. I motioned him over to the table to sit with us and introduced him to the rest of the table. "This is Sammy. He's a homeboy from Atlantic City."

Big Stan, who was about six five and was serving twenty years, said "Homey or not, I'm going to get some of that. Ain't no guns in here to protect him." Before I could say anything, Big Hawk and several of the older homeys told Stan he was not going to do anything to this boy. They warned him if he did, there was going to be trouble. At that point, I told Sammy whatever score we had to settle in the streets was forgotten now. That was behind us once we came to the penitentiary. He could relax as far as he and I were concerned. We stick together in the joint. I told him if he stood up for himself, the rest of us would stand up for him. E, who was an old-timer, chimed in and said, "That's right, young blood. I'll get you a shank in the morning. You've got to protect yourself." It wasn't long before Stan put in a transfer on Sammy's behalf to 1 Right where the kitchen workers were housed. Before Sammy knew it, he was being transferred.

During the noon meal, one of the kitchen workers passed me a note saying that they conspired with my homeboy Stan to get him transferred and that they were planning to rape Sammy that night. This was not unusual. It was a common practice in prison to get a specific guard to leave your cell door open and allow things to happen. I told Sammy the safest thing he could do to protect himself at this point was to ask to be put in protective custody, which he did. From there, he was later shipped to a reformatory to finish out the remainder of his sentence with his manhood left intact.

About a month later, three friends I had run with from time to time—Pinky, Nail Head, and Brian—came in with life sentences. They robbed a jewelry store and killed a man in the process. I was just grateful that I had already been serving my six-year sentence because I could have easily been with them. Weeks later, two brothers who were friends of mine were shipped in from the reformatory for beating up a couple of guards and starting a riot. They had been in and out of jail most of their lives. When they were kids, a man killed their mother and they vowed to one another that they would keep trying to get to the prison with the man who killed their mother. It seemed that they had gotten their wish. However, when they arrived, they were disappointed to find that he had been shipped to another prison years before. The last thing I heard, they were doing six or seven life sentences in a federal prison somewhere. The man who killed their mother has long since been released and died of natural cause on the streets.

13

RAHWAY AND LEESBURG

After spending about two years back behind the wall, I was shipped to Rahway. There I witnessed gang rapes, brutal beatings, and a variety of ingenious prison-run extortion rackets. I was to lock on 4 Right. My job was the head shop hall runner. I was to pick up the count slips in the morning from the various prison shops which gave a count of how many inmates each shop had working or were absent, running errands, and helping to unload trucks that came in with prison supplies. This meant I was moving all over the penitentiary. This enabled me to hustle contraband such as shanks, money, and dope from the shops to the blocks. I only had two Atlantic City homeboys there, so we didn't even have a special table at Rahway like we did at in Trenton.

At that time, they recently abolished the death penalty in New Jersey. When the guys were released from death row, they kept some in Trenton. Others came to Rahway because their sentences had been commuted to life. The guys who came out of death row took a liking to me because I was young, wild, and foolish. I was allowed to sit at the table with these guys who had been on death row. They thought somehow they could keep me from getting in a lot of unnecessary trouble. Now that I look back on it, they did at times. I would spend most of my time reading, playing chess and handball, talking, and learning from an old card shark named Black Joe. Black Joe killed a man with a knife in a crap game. He also had a reputation in the prison for cutting up some convicts who disrespected him. He was very quiet, mild-mannered, and dangerous. He also sat at the death-row table. Of all places, Black Joe also worked in the machine shop where most of the prison shanks were made. I never felt I would need one.

One day, Big Mac and I were playing handball on the yard. Most of the time, I would beat him, talk smack, and embarrass him in front of the other convicts. I admit sometimes I would take it a little too far. Coming in from the yard, Big Mac crossed the line and punk-slapped me (slap with back of hand). He said, "What you going to do now?"

Before I could respond, some inmates came between us. I told him he hadn't seen the last of this and that he could bet on it. I tried to get a shank from the machine shop the next day. For some reason, I couldn't get one so I slipped a claw hammer out undetected. Since I was the head shop-hall runner, I was never searched going back to the wing. I locked on 4 Right; Big Mac locked on 4 Left. When it was time for our wing to be called for chow, one side would be let out first and then about ten or fifteen minutes later, the other side would be let out.

This particular day, 4 Right (my side) would be let out first for chow. I went around to the other side where Mac locked and waited for his cell door to open to catch him by surprise. It was my lucky day! When the doors were opened, I rushed into his cell to find him sitting on the toilet. I commenced to beat him with the hammer. I hit him in the head and shoulders as he tried to cover himself while on the toilet stool. Other inmates tried to pull me off of him. The death-row inmates were the ones who got the hammer out of my hands and moved me quickly off the wing. "I told you I was going to get you back, didn't I?" I said as they pulled me away.

In the meantime, I heard other convicts saying to one another, "I told Mac he had better watch that young joker." As for Mac, he survived with only a few stitches to his head and some scars. Big Mac never told who did this to him or did anyone else. If the powers that be had known it was me that had done this to Mac, they probably would not have said anything to me about it anyway. As I look back, maybe the reason no one said anything about it was because of who my escorts were in the prison. The death-row inmates I sat with at the table always tried to keep me out of trouble the best they could.

The rest of my time in Rahway went pretty smoothly until about a year later when I decided I would take a barbering class that was being offered to the inmates. I thought that I might become a barber once I was released. The class was held in one of the two barbershops in the prison. One barbershop was outside with the other shops but this one was located just before entering the chow hall opposite the commissary. This class met about twice a week with an instructor who would teach us things about hair and scalp, how to hold the clippers and scissors, and what blades to use. I was learning pretty well, I thought, and I paid attention to the instructor. The time came when we could invite someone to our chair if they dared to take the risk with the instructor supervising us as we did the cutting. The rest of the guys in the class had homeys who would allow them to practice on their heads under the supervision of the instructor. All I could do was watch the others cut since no one would dare sit in my chair. The weeks went on, and I had no one to sit in my chair. I grew desperate. I felt that the rest of the class was getting ahead of me and I was getting left behind. I felt that I had to do something radical to get someone in my chair if I was going to keep up with the rest of the class.

One night, one of the wings were making commissary. As the inmates stood in line waiting to get their commissary, I stood in the doorway of the barbershop wearing a starched, shiny, white barbering jacket with scissors in hand, looking like a busy barber just taking a break in between cuts. As I scanned the line, I noticed a short, muscular man who looked like he needed a cut. I later found out that they called him Nitro. "Say, brother, I see you look like you might be needing my expertise. Why don't you step over here after you get your commissary and let me touch you up a bit before I get busy again?" I offered.

"Okay!" he said, "I'll give you a try when I get finished." Once I got Nitro in my chair, I started off like a pro but then I got a bit scissor-happy and cut a little too much off the top. While trying to straighten it out before he would notice, he saw one of the barbers snickering. "Hey, what you doing, now?" he said while looking in the mirror.

I replied, "Don't worry, man. I got you. If I mess up, we have an instructor here who can straighten it out."

"What? You mean to tell me you're just learning how to cut? I thought you knew what you were doing?" he said as he pulled the apron off, jumping out of the chair.

I said, "Calm down, man. It ain't that bad."

He was angry, "Naw, man! Now we're going to fight. You messed my head up!"

At this point, I hoped that someone would talk him down since I still held the scissors in my hand. I wanted to avoid the violence at all costs, which would surely take place if the situation escalated. Fortunately, the instructor took him to the side and reasoned with him. He assured him if he would just calm down, he would finish cutting his hair himself. He convinced him that it wasn't so bad and that I was to go back to my wing. The next day, I was given a notice from the instructor not to return to the class.

In the months that followed, I took the test for my GED for the second time and finally passed. This was the only positive thing that I had accomplished during my incarceration. I felt that I needed a change of scenery so I put in for a transfer to go back to Leesburg where I'd be closer to home and could catch up on the latest news from Atlantic City. Within months, I was on a prison transfer bus back to Leesburg. Once again, my job assignment would be back in the tag shop making New Jersey license plates. In the evenings, I had taken some courses that were being offered at the Mercer county college. I joined a study group with eight other guys. We studied together in the evenings. I did rather well and was quite proud of myself.

I was later transferred to the prison farm that housed about five hundred inmates. I was now winding down my sentence. Inmates would hurry to finish eating to gather under a large tree to listen and laugh while Tootsie and Moco would go back and forth telling tall tales that would keep us all laughing. Tootsie would tell about the time he had flown in one Sunday in a helicopter with its propellers blowing everyone's food off the tables while landing and how he had made up for it by serving everybody shrimp and lobster out of the back of the helicopter. Moco would tell about how he had once swam around the English Channel, and later become the first black underwater frogman. Tootsie would try and go one better by telling about having six Chinese maids when people would come to his home. When you would ring his doorbell, one maid would call his name, "Tootsie, Tootsie, Tootsie!" Another would answer the door. These guys would sit around and tell flat-out lies for entertainment, sometimes laughing at themselves. Sometimes inmates would toss them packs of cigarettes just for having made them laugh.

14

STREETOLOGIST

In June 1974, I was finally released from the New Jersey State penitentiary system at twenty-five years old. I was armed with a GED, a few college credits in one hand, and, most importantly, a PhD in *Streetology* in the other. I was ready to make my claim to fame. However, during the first two weeks I was out, I decided I wouldn't rush getting back into the swing of things since I had been incarcerated for so many years.

In the evenings, I would stand outside of Brodie's Pool Room on Kentucky Avenue and look up the street and see the infamous Club Harlem. I could hear the music of Chris Columbo's band on one side of the street, and on the other side was Grace's Little Belmont where Sammy Davis Jr.'s mother worked for many years as a barmaid. Next to that was Golden's Bar, which was owned by a fellow named Catfish who was later killed while trying to break up a fight in his own bar. If I looked to the right, on the corner of Kentucky and Arctic was the Wondergarden owned by Sonny McCall, which featured singers like the Isley Brothers; Earth, Wind & Fire, the Four Tops, and others. Next to the pool hall was an alley leading to another smaller alley that led to a door where men and women would gather in a smoke-filled room to place their bets in a game of Georgia Skin. Later, traffic got more congested as people made their way from one joint to the next. Luxury cars would drive by as pimps and hustlers moved through the streets. A parade of fast ladies of the night would just be coming out while their pimps would give them their last-minute instructions for the evening. This was a world of its own. This was my world, a world that had seduced me and turned me out while shining shoes as a kid on this same street many years ago.

It wasn't long before things started coming together for me. I would make my rounds from pool hall to pool hall, the gambling houses, and night spots. People were glad to see me out. Someone would always put a piece of money in my hand, telling me how good I looked and how they were glad to see me home. The pimps would give you money to buy a few outfits to help you catch up, the hustlers would give you money so you would have a bank for hustling, and the drug dealer would give you dope to get high. However, I decided that I would abstain from all mood altering substances. I was determined to stay focused and not get sidetracked with the dumb stuff.

About a week later, Nubfingers found me standing outside the pool hall gazing. When he pulled up, he honked the horn and shouted, "Where your mind at, man?" I looked up to see him sitting in his forest-green Cadillac grinning like a Cheshire cat. "Where you been, man?" he asked.

I answered, "I've been out over two weeks. I'm just now seeing you."

He said, "I've been on the road. I just got off the road this morning with Fats. Get in the car. You got some money?" Before I could answer, he was putting two one-hundred-dollar bills in my hand. "I've got some stuff I won off a mark in a gambling game. If you think you can do something with it, I'll give it to you."

"Thanks, Nub," I said.

Then he went to his trunk, rummaging around in an old pile of clothes. He pulled out a shopping bag half full of what appeared to be marijuana. He said, "Man, this ain't your average weed. They call this stuff wacky weed because if you smoke it, it'll make you wacky. If you can sell this stuff, you can make you some money to get on your feet. In fact, you don't even have to put that much in a bag and still get ten dollars a bag for this stuff."

I told Nubby to take me uptown to a little storefront joint. My father gave me a key to it when I got home because it had one shine stand. He said I could do something with it one day once I got on my feet because he wasn't doing anything with it. He also gave me the key to the apartment that sat atop the storefront. I stashed this wacky weed there until I could buy some bags to bag it up. I made a few inquiries to find out who would smoke this kind of stuff. It wasn't long before people all over town were looking for me, trying to buy this stuff. It wasn't long before I ran out of it and cashed in my earnings for half an ounce of coke.

Several times, I went on the road with Nubby hustling pool, cards, and dice. Nubby was not just your average, run-of-the-mill hustler. He was a card shark, pool shark, and shrewd businessman. He also owned a grocery store in one of the most notorious Hispanic sections in the city. Although he owned a Cadillac, he never wash it, except on special occasions because he was careful not to draw any attention to himself. Whenever he transported dope, he would always drive the metered cab he owned. Nubby would never wear clothes or jewelry that would draw undue attention to himself. He was a master of disguise and very cunning.

15

LEGITIMATE BUSINESSMAN

I t wasn't long before I was on my feet in full swing with an entourage that sold drugs, love, and hot goods. It was Nubfingers who encouraged me to open the storefront my father offered to me. He said it would be smart to open up a legitimate business in order to justify the illegitimate money I was making, especially since I didn't have a job to account for the kind of money I had. I purchased a mercantile license, bought a candy case for candy, and put in an ice cream box for my ice cream, a cash register for the counter, a soda box for sodas, a cigarette machine, and one shine stand that would sit in the front bay window along with a boot block. To top it off, I got a hot dog rotisserie and became known for the best hot dogs and sausages in town. I decided to call it Reggie's Confectionary and Novelty Store and paid a professional sign painter to put it on the front window for a few bags of dope.

I was now a legitimate businessman and business was rather good. The Pennsylvania Avenue schoolyard was across the street where guys would play pick-up basketball nightly during the summer. There would always be crowds of people around the fence and inside on bleachers to watch the game and cheer for their favorite team. Others would make wagers as to what team would win or what player would score the most points. My store was the closest and most convenient to come for a cold drink, sausage, or hot dog. We kept a steady flow of business with six spots a day on the radio advertising. "The best sausages and hot dogs in town!" I paid a local deejay on the weekends to spin records at a local club that I leased to have dances for teenagers from 9:00 p.m. to 12:00 a.m.

I lived in a tenth floor apartment at an exclusive highrise building on the boardwalk. My front window from the tenth floor overlooked the entire city, and it was most beautiful at night. Despite living large and having money, I was missing one thing. I didn't know how to drive or have a driver's license. Up until this point, I was always jumping in and out of cabs. I had certain cab drivers I used to get around to take care of my business. Before long, luck smiled on me and sent me another helperdriving a Cadillac with the three *B*s—beauty, brains, and business.

She cut into me using the pretense that she had just closed up her business and was looking for a new business location downtown. She was sharp and knew her stuff. She made it known from the onset that she was competing for the first place spot in my entourage. She didn't waste any time either, saying, "Whenever you need to go somewhere, I want you to call me so that I can take you. You don't need to be calling no cab to take you nowhere when you got me." So I decided to take her up on it and had her pick me up when I was ready to go instead of taking a cab. One particular night when she was driving me, she popped the proverbial question, "Do you want to drive?"

I was startled. I didn't know whether to piss in my pants or jump out of the car and start running. "No, I don't want to drive. I like it better when you drive," I said.

Then came the next question. "Reggie, can you drive?"

Not wanting to sound completely clueless, I said, "Well, a little, not much."

"Do you want me to teach you how to drive?" she offered.

"This car is too big for me to learn how to drive. Maybe if we had a smaller car, I could learn."

She said, "No, baby, I can teach you how to drive in this car. Come on, baby, let me teach you how to drive. I'm going to pull over and let you get behind the wheel. You'll do good."

That night, I got behind the wheel of a Cadillac and Nesy began teaching me to drive. Although Nesy taught me how to drive—among other things and was very good to me—she could never compete with Linda who would prove to be the best lady friend a man could ever have in his corner. She came up in the same public housing projects as I had, struggling trying to get a dollar out of a dime. She was the oldest of four girls and fast beyond her years. Life left her a widow with three children, and she had a marijuana business to make ends meet. We started off doing business together. As time went on, a relationship developed between us. She was wise in business, which was good for me. I could trust her with large sums of money as well as drugs. She would open up my store at the crack of dawn and would stay most of the day making sure that my business was being managed well. Occasionally, she would buy gifts and groceries for my Ocean Manor apartment. She kept an immaculate house of her own, which was a great place to get away from it all while listening to the melodious sounds of Minnie Ripperton, the Isley Brothers, or some other group. This was where I would bring many of my business associates to discuss plans over a good meal, good music, and good drugs. My privacy was always safely guarded. Whenever friends or business associates would come in from out of town, they would always check with Linda regarding my whereabouts. Whenever I was out of town for periods of time, she would handle all of my affairs as if I was right there. I was careful never to keep large amounts of drugs at her house.

One night while we were both minding the store, the police raided the house looking for a large amount of drugs, which they didn't find. All they found was some marijuana. One of the kids called the store that night to inform us that the house had been raided. The police had found something and they had a warrant for Linda's arrest. They also said the police tore up the house pretty badly. It was a mess. We decided she would stay away from the house that night until I could hire an attorney to go with her the following day to post the bond so that she would not have to see the inside of a jail cell. She also did not want to see her house in the mess the police had left. We got some friends to go over, sit with the kids, and clean up the mess. I held her in safekeeping for the rest of the night. Although she never did a day in jail for these charges as I had promised her, she did get a five-year probation with a strong reprimand from the judge to never come before him again or else she would most certainly be going to prison. Truly, they really wanted me. Even though she got probation, these charges would haunt her for the next thirty-five years.

Nubfingers warned me I was drawing too much attention to myself when I had went against his advice and bought a beautiful 1966 Cadillac Coupe Deville. It was eight years old, had one owner, in mint condition, and was white with a black vinyl top. Even though Nubby advised against it, I just couldn't resist. I reasoned that it wasn't a new Cadillac like some of my other friends were driving since it was eight years old. Nub and a lot of the older hustlers didn't believe in a lot of flash, pomp, bling, and glitter. They thought that was for suckers wanting attention, but we were different. We were players personified. We were supposed to be smarter than that. We were supposed to have more going for us with more things to do to get money than just selling drugs. We did a variety of things and didn't have to sell drugs all the time. We were crap players, pool hustlers, card sharks, and confidence men who took our crafts serious.

I began paying for my choice because the police were now following my pretty white Cadillac and watching my every move. They could see the car when they couldn't see me. Nubfingers and others began to shy away from me because I was drawing too much attention. They didn't want to come by my store because they thought the police were sitting in a car or a building somewhere with a pair of binoculars watching my every move. They didn't want to call me because they thought the police might have my phone bugged. They would only deal with me when we would go out of town to play cards, craps, or the confidence game. Once back in town, they would stay clear of me. Often, I was gone on the road hustling for weeks at a time and I could always depend on Linda to have my affairs in order when I returned.

Nesy was disappointed in me because she thought that I should have bought a Cadillac like hers. She would say, "After all, that's what you learned to drive in." Near my twenty-seventh birthday, Nesy said that she was working on my birthday present. She said she almost finished with the paperwork on it and that she hoped to have everything in order within a few days so that she could present me with my gift. A few days later, she called me to come over because she had my present ready and I had to sign some papers before I could take possession of it. I just knew she had gone ahead and bought a Cadillac for me. What else could it be? I rushed to her house as fast as I could. When I pulled up, I didn't see it in front of the house. I went in, and she said that we would go and get it because people had it waiting for me. I thought, *That figures, it's still on the car lot.* Once we got into her car, she hands me some papers to a very fine breed of Doberman pinscher. The owner had one left in the litter. She bred these dogs from Germany. Nesy went on and on about the dog's mother, father, and the bloodline.

This wasn't what I had in mind and I went nuts. "You mean to tell me you brought me out here to give me a dog? Are you crazy? Have you lost your mind?" I already had one dog that was a malamute husky that shed hair all over the furniture. I needed another dog like I needed a hole in the head. However, I decided to name this dog Negroe and added gunpowder to his diet to make him a mean and viscous killer. His job was to discourage the police or any would-be intruder who might plan to come in on me. When I tried to add two more Dobermans to assist Negroe in his job, within three days, I found them both dead. He was too mean for helpers.

One day, a police officer and his drug dog came into my store. The officer pretended to be a customer who wanted a sausage and a drink. While the new girl working behind the counter was preparing his order, he told her what he wanted. "Put lots of mustard on it and some onions and a little bit of ketchup," he said as he casually dropped the leash, allowing the dog to wander and sniff for some drugs. Suddenly, the dog darted behind my counter and frightened the girl that was working. She screamed.

The dog then came to the door leading to the back of the store where Negroe's headquarters were, running back out as quickly as he had gone in. Negroe was behind him and looked like he had seen a ghost. I jumped off the shine stand I was sitting on, watching the whole episode go down. I grabbed my dog as the police officer was trying to catch up with his dog that was trying to paw his way through the front door. This was one of many attempts by the police to try and catch me, although I didn't think that I was that big to warrant so much attention.

The girl behind the counter had only been working a couple of days on a trial basis. When my younger brother came through the store the day before and saw her behind the counter, he pulled me aside and told me that she might be a bit young to work in this type of traffic. She was about his age and going to school with him. I looked at him as if he had two heads in disbelief. "You mean to tell me that this girl went to school with you? I don't believe it. This girl is much older than you," I said.

He was adamant. "Now, bro, I'm telling you, check it out."

That evening, I asked her about it and she assured me that she was much older. I still wasn't quiet convinced so I asked her not to come back around until she brought me her birth certificate. She assured me she would. The following evening, she was back working when I came in. Linda put her behind the counter as she did the day before because she was not aware of the birth certificate conversation. She didn't know I pulled the girl from behind the counter until I got a copy of her birth certificate. The girl said that she had not been able to find it. I told her again that I couldn't have her working in my store without that birth certificate. I explained to her that I was doing a lot of things that were against the law. She was young, wanting to be hip and a part of this operation, but I couldn't take any chances. "You will draw more heat on me than I care to have. When you get your birth certificate, you can come back." The following day, she was back again. "Didn't I tell you not to come back until you had your birth certificate?" I said.

"I still couldn't find it but my mother told me to tell you that she is my birth certificate. Go talk to her."

Since she was so persistent, I decided that I would march her around the corner to her mother who lived in the block next to my store. I knocked on the door with the girl beside me. Once the mother came to the door, I told her how persistent her daughter was in wanting to work at my store but I needed to see a birth certificate. "She couldn't produce one. Now she tells me that you said you are her birth certificate," I said.

Her mother nodded and agreed. She said, "My daughter is of age, you have nothing to worry about. She has misplaced her birth certificate."

I asked her mother, "Do you know who I am?" She said she did. "Then I guess you are well aware of all that I do. I do some illegal stuff. Although I have a store, there are some illegal things that take place there sometimes. Are you all right with that?" I asked.

"You don't have to worry about me, and my daughter can take care of herself," she replied.

16

BUSTED AND
ALMOST BUSTED

A few days later, I had just returned from New York with a lot of dope to cut up, package, and put on the streets. It was about three in the morning and too late to take it all to one of my out of the way stashes. I decided I would call the young girl from my store to meet me in front of her building around the corner from the store.

As I pulled up to her building, she came down the stairs and got into my car. I told her I had a lot of dope on me and I needed her to stash it for me until later that day so that I could go get some rest. As I sat in the car giving her instructions, a police detective pulled up behind me and one along side of me. Normally, I would pass the drugs to the female and let her stash it or take the weight for it, but something told me I better not do that. This was against all my training and street smarts. I held on to the dope in my lap and told her to get out of the car and run up the steps. She said that she wasn't moving and she wanted me to give her the dope. I refused. She insisted, begging me to give her the drugs. All of my instincts told me not to do it.

The detective approached the car, saw that it was me, and asked me to get out. The drugs were visible in my lap. I didn't even try to hide them. It was hopeless. He was so excited about catching me he couldn't wait until morning light to call his superior. He phoned him at home while standing in front of me with handcuffs on. "Chief, sorry to wake you this time of the morning, but you won't guess who I got red-handed. Reggie Longcrier! It's a big one!"

They took us both to the station that morning. I cautioned the girl not to say anything. "You don't know nothing about no drugs," I told her.

While they had both of us in the room, a detective began to grill her. "What's your name?"

"Diane."

"Where do you live?"

"North Carolina Avenue."

"How old are you?"

"Seventeen."

My instinct had been right to not give her the drugs! In the meantime, her older sister was out front fighting with officers and trying to get in. She was screaming because she knew how the game went down. "If he thinks my sister is going to take the weight for him, he's got another thing coming!" She didn't know how wrong she was. They allowed her to come into the office.

The girl sadly told her older sister, "No, sis, that's not right. He wouldn't let me take it. He wouldn't give it to me."

The next day, the girl's mother got the news that I wouldn't let her daughter take the weight for me and that I had cut her loose. She sent word to me that she was sorry she had lied about her daughter's age and that if I was going to have any repercussions because of it, she was willing to talk to the authorities to vindicate me. However, there was no need for that. The police were more than happy to just get me with some drugs.

I made bond and was out the following day. The case was continued several times. I didn't really face the court over these charges until years later because as my drug addiction escalated, I left town to avoid prosecution in hopes that a geographic change would solve my problems. I was always running away from myself. The biggest problem I had was wherever I went, I always took me along. The same problems followed me no matter where I went.

Days after getting out of jail, my friend Bev was calling me from North Jersey where she had been visiting her mother for a few days. She was a booster who specialized in stealing high-dollar men and women's clothing. She worked the North Jersey area while she was visiting her mother and had fifteen to twenty garbage bags full of hot clothes ready to be brought back to Atlantic City and sold. Fats said that he would ride with me to pick her up since he wasn't doing anything. Plus, he wanted to convince me it was time for me to leave Atlantic City again for a while to hustle craps, cards, and pool. Fats told me it was time to hang up the drug game. I was getting too hot. It was just a matter of time before I would be on my way back to prison. Even worse, I began using my own product again.

That evening, we picked up Bev from her mother's house in North Jersey and loaded the car with large, black garbage bags full of hot clothing with the tags still on them. When we couldn't fill the empty trunk anymore so we filled the entire back seat until there was no more room. The three of us now headed back to Atlantic City squeezed in the front seat while carrying thousands of dollars' worth of hot clothes. We traveled down the dark roads late that Sunday night, talking and figuring what fence would take the whole load off our hands and give us the price we wanted. All of a sudden, smoke started coming out of the hood of my car.

Fats told me to pull over. "Let me take a look under the hood."

Fats knew more about fixing cars than any brother I had ever known. I used to be amazed at how much he knew, since he was always known to drive nothing but new Cadillacs. When I would ask him about it, he would boast about having nine hundred hours of auto mechanics training under his belt from when he was in prison fixing state cars. Once he popped the hood, he quickly discovered we had a busted radiator. One of the neighbors saw three black figures moving in the dark near their home and called the police. Soon three police cars show up. Here we were, three crooks with a car load of hot goods and a busted radiator, just right for going to jail.

The first two officers approached the car, shining flashlights in our faces. "What's the trouble?" they asked. Fats said, "Looks like we have a busted radiator, officer. Do you know of any place that can fix this, sir?"

They answered, "No, not this time of night, but we can have it towed to one of the local shops and they can take a look at it in the morning." The other officer asked us where we were headed.

I said, "We're headed to Atlantic City, sir. We were helping this lady move. The moving truck has already gone ahead with her furniture, and we were helping move her clothes since they couldn't get anything else on the truck."

As they flashed the light in the car, one officer said to the other, "Sure is a lot of clothes."

I said, "Yes, sir. She's even got her kids clothes in bags in the trunk. I guess she didn't want to leave nothing."

While this was going on, Fats was talking to the other officers and telling them that his daddy used to be a policeman, how he used to ride him in his police cruiser when he was a boy and he used to let him turn on the siren. One officer asked him where his daddy served on the force. "Philadelphia, sir," he replied.

"Is he still serving?" the officer asked.

"No, sir," Fats answered. "He was killed in the line of duty."

One officer apologized while the others shook their heads in sympathy. Fats told them we were needing to get to Atlantic City and asked if they would do like his dad did while serving on the police force. Fats explained back then if someone was stranded and needed to get to the next county, they would call a 10-20. They all looked at one another in astonishment, surprised that Fats would know so much about how the police operated. He went on reciting other codes he remembered from when his father was on the force. Soon, Fats had this officer calling in a 10-20—or whatever the call numbers were—for police in the county ahead. They informed them that they were bringing us to that county line so that the police there could get us to the next county line. So with the help of these fine police officers, we unloaded the bags from the trunk and the back seat of my car into one of the police cruisers, both trunk and back seat, with the police taking us to the next county line. Another patrol car from the next county carried us to the neighboring county, bags and all!

We did this throughout the night with police escorts who took us through about eight to ten counties until we got back to Atlantic City. Not one officer ever asked to look into our bags to see what we were carrying. Fats had been *BS*ing the police with this jive about his daddy having been a police officer killed in the line of duty. I was amazed how much he knew to make his story so believable to those unsuspecting officers. I don't remember asking him how he knew so much about the police. I was so happy we didn't go to jail that night I just didn't think to ask. Although I had made a nice piece of money after selling all of the merchandise to a fence, life always has a way of catching up with you, making you pay for your wrongs.

About a month later, I was in Washington D.C. Gene and I had just loaded the trunk of my car full with slum watches and rings. They were all prepared in beautiful boxes with price tag stickers ready to be sold. We gassed up the Caddy and headed to Newport News, Virginia, home of the Washington Avenue shipyard. This was the time of month when the shipyard workers would get paid and hundreds of shipyard workers would be cashing their checks. Slum hustlers would be waiting to unload their wares. Once Gene and I arrived in town, we met up with my old partner D.D. who was now living in Richmond with his girlfriend, an elementary school teacher. We met in a local restaurant with D.D. and a few guys that he had been working with who had come in town from Philadelphia. I knew them from the past and I remembered these guys were very serious about their craft. They all drove Cadillacs, dressed neatly, and didn't drink or drug. During lunch, we'd talk shop about slum shops, slum prices, and the various kinds of new slum pieces that were out. Then we hit the streets. We met back up in the evening to see who had sold the most or made the most money for the day. I left the restaurant, giving Gene the keys to the car while he continued finishing his food. I told him to catch up with me later with the car because I was headed up the block. Before Gene could catch up with me, he had hit on two or three people. Apparently, one had called the police describing the car he was driving. When Gene found me, I got into the driver's seat while Gene went into a small grocery store on the corner to get a cold drink.

Minutes later, two detectives pulled up alongside me, asking to see my driver's license and registration. After showing them my license and registration, they then asked to look in the trunk of my car. I opened the trunk full of watches and rings that we had stocked up, ready for sale. They opened the boxes and saw the $300 to $1,000-price tag stickers, which we had placed on the watches and rings. By this time, a large crowd gathered to see what was going on. "Where did you steal this stuff from? We just got a call you were selling a lot of stuff around here," they said.

"No, sir," I said. "This stuff ain't hot. I've got receipts for everything I have here, sir." I pulled out the receipts.

After they had looked over all my receipts, they began to incite the crowd by telling them that we were from the big city and that we thought that the good folks in Newport News, Virginia, were suckers. "They think we're dumb around here. Why don't we just run 'em out of town."

A voice then came from the crowd, "Yeah, let's run 'em out of town!" The crowd began to chant, "Run 'em out of town! Run 'em out of town! Run 'em out of town!".

While the crowd was chanting, one of the detectives turned to me and asked where my partner was. He looked around to scan the crowd for a face that looked like the face on Gene's driver's license, which he had gotten out of the trunk in some clothes. Even though Gene was in the crowd, I believe the reason he couldn't identify him was because Gene was shouting with the rest of the crowd, "Run 'em out of town! Run 'em out of town!"

By this time, the other officer had written up an itemized list of watches and rings that he had taken from my trunk along with all of my money, with the exception of a small stash I had kept in my shoe. "Here, this is your receipt for the stuff we're confiscating from you. You come back here

Monday for your stuff and make sure you got bail money when you come back because you'll need it."

My receipt had been torn from a page in the back of the officer's address book. I knew then that these crooked cops intended to keep my stuff and really didn't expect me to come back for it. By this time, they had summoned for two cruisers to lead me to the city line, one in front and one behind me. I left Gene to get back to Washington the best way he could while I was headed to Norfolk. I had no more watches or rings to sell, and most of my money was gone. I decided I would try and shortchange a few stores to build my bank back up and then go back to D.C. to replace the stock that was taken from me. However, just as I was entering the city limits of Norfolk, I was pulled over by Norfolk's finest. "What's the problem, officer?" I asked as he approached my car.

"Get out of the car and put your hands across the hood."

I did as I was told as he shook me down, removing my money and my wallet from my pockets. "What's going on?" I asked.

"A woman who works at the clam store in Ocean View called us and said that a man driving a Cadillac fitting your description came through her place. After you left, her register was short."

I said, "Sir, this must be some mistake because I would have no reason to take any money from anybody's store. I'm in business myself. I have a store of my own. I know all too well the hassles of running a store. Far be it from me to do anything like that. You can check me out. My store is in Atlantic City, New Jersey."

The officer said, "Well, we're going to hold on to you until she comes to identify you."

They carried me straight to the city jail and locked me up. After about four hours of sitting in a jail cell not knowing what my next move would be or how long I'd be in for, I hear the clanging of keys and my cell door opening. A big, burly officer told me that I was free to go. "Boy, it seems like this is your lucky day. The woman that was supposed to identify you is sailing to another navy base with her husband in the morning. She won't be around for court so we have to let you go." Two officers escorted me to where my car had been parked with a boot on it to keep me from leaving town until they were ready for me to leave. They unlocked the boot, told me to leave town, and not be seen in their town again.

After two close calls in one day, it was time to quit for the day so I headed back to D.C. By the time I got to Richmond, I was exhausted. I rented a room for the night to rest and gather my thoughts. The next morning, I woke up fresh and feeling rested. I decided that I would break luck by short-changing a few of the local stores in Richmond before leaving in order to replenish my bank and to help make up for the loss that I had suffered the day before. Gene was far better at this than I was, although I had taught him how to do it years before while we were in prison with monopoly money. Once I was back in D.C., I drove to Gene's apartment on Pennsylvania Avenue Southeast. Much to my surprise, he was already home. "How did you get back?" I asked.

"I made it to the bus station and slipped out of town on the first thing smoking," he said.

After working the D.C. area a few days, I headed to New York and checked into a hotel on 135th Street in Harlem. Shortly after I was there, I got news from Atlantic City that Nubfingers was killed by two men that I had known in prison. Rumor was that Nubfingers had been in his apartment upstairs while Sorefeet minded his grocery store below. Two men came in carrying machete knives and forced Sorefeet to open the cash register and hand them the money. After that, they forced Sorefeet up the stairs that led to the apartment where Nubfingers and his sister from Detroit were visiting. Once they forced their way into the apartment, they tied them all up in chairs with their hands behind their backs. After they got all the money that was in the house, they cut them up one by one while they pleaded for their lives. They killed Nubfinger's sister first, then Nubfinger. Sorefeet was the only survivor of this tragedy. Years later, he confided in me that the only reason he lived that day was because by the time they finished cutting up Nubfingers and his sister, the knife was too dull. He carried scars on his body and a large gash across his throat as a reminder of that tragic night.

17

GOING DOWN IN NEW YORK

A few months later, Cee Cee, whose father was a city official, bugged me to let her come to New York and work the streets. For some reason, she had a fascination with being a bad girl and needed to prove that she wasn't square. I let her come to New York, which I would later regret for many years. After some time on the streets, she got sick so I tried to convince her to go back home. She told me that was the last thing she wanted to do and was very adamant about it. I told her she couldn't stay with me sick like that and that she needed to decide where she wanted to go. She told me before that she had an aunt in New York but she really didn't want to go there unless she had to. I convinced her to let me take her there. Once we got there, she changed her mind.

After all I had gone through to convince her to pack her bags to go and driving her all the way to Queens in a thunderstorm, now she wants to change her mind. I don't know whether it was the rain or the cocaine that I had been shooting that made me so impatient with her. I ended up going to my trunk and tossing out all of her bags that I helped her pack. I put her out of my car, drove off into the night, and left her standing in the rain—bags and all. The drugs were beginning to take its toll on me. When I looked in the mirror, I saw a man I had not seen in years—cold, insensitive, and relentless. I didn't care about anything but the next fix. If I had any second thoughts about leaving Cee Cee that night in the rain, they were only fleeting. The cocaine dulled my senses. I had no emotion.

About two months later, an older hustler by the name of Cuda and I had just gotten through cornering a couple of construction workers into a game of three-card monte. After dividing our winnings, we headed uptown to Harlem to cop some dope and a few peewee caps of cocaine that we heard Black Ernie had on 117th Street and Eighth Avenue. We parked the car on 119th Street and walked back to 117th Street. As we were walking, I heard the pitter-patter of light footsteps coming fast behind us. *Oh no, this can't be the police! We haven't even copped yet. It must be some stick-up boys*, I thought.

It's a good thing I stashed most of my money in my socks and had just enough in my pockets to cop with. I knew Cuda had enough sense to do the same. As the footsteps got closer, we both turned around to see a short, small-framed woman hollering at the top of her lungs, "Where's Cee Cee?" Another taller, dark-skinned woman ran across the street to catch up, out of breath. She asked, "Yeah, we want to know what you've done with Cee Cee!"

I said that I hadn't seen Cee Cee in months. The dark-skinned one then said that she had last been seen with me. They believed that I must have done something to her. They went on to say that she hadn't called home for her birthday last month. It was not like her to miss calling home on her birthday every year regardless of where she was. The short one then said, "If you've done something to her, you haven't heard the last of this."

Not wanting to seem worried, I said, "Well, she's old enough to be wherever she wants to be, and she'll probably be found whenever she wants to be found."

Cuda then pulled me aside and said, "Come on, man. Let's go on and do what we come up here for. You ain't got time to be arguing with these women."

After we had copped our drugs, we went to a friend of Cuda's who lived on Lennox Avenue. He allowed us to use some syringes for a taste or a fee. Once I had gotten off on the dope, I just couldn't seem to shake thinking about what might have happened to Cee Cee. A week later, I had blown my money on some bad dope. Broke and down on my luck, I decided that I would go around to the Shalamar on 123rd and Seventh Avenue. I probably could get some money from my homeboy Iceman.

Iceman had gotten his name after coming home from the Bordentown Reformatory in New Jersey. When he was released, he hustled up enough money to buy an old man's ice truck business delivering ice to stores for their soda boxes. Although it was a dying business and the days of buying blocks of ice were just about over, Iceman had a knack for selling ice to people who didn't need any ice. It was often said that he could probably sell ice to Eskimos. Now he was a limousine-driving pimp, just as cold as the ice he had once sold. Iceman had been in New York a couple of years now and had done rather well for himself. On my way to see him, my mind went back to when I had known him years ago. We had gotten tight back when I was a teenager. Iceman was selling marijuana at the time along with selling ice. Back then, I bought a nickel bag from Iceman to split with another kid that had served time with me in the reformatory.

That particular day, we both had to report to our parole officer. When we were a block away from the parole office, it dawned on me that I had the bag of marijuana in my pocket.

I asked Butch whether I should take the risk of going in with the bag of weed. Butch replied, "Here, hand it here. I'll hold it."

Once I gave the bag to Butch, I watched him put it in his sock. "Hey, I could have done that. Give me that bag back. I'll just put it in my sock," I said.

After some fencing back and forth, it was decided that I would hold the weed in my sock. Butch and I sat in the lobby of the parole office waiting for our names to be called. After some time, they called me first. "Longcrier, Mr. Davenport will see you now."

When I stepped in the office, there sitting next to Mr. Davenport was a familiar face, Tom Davis. He was a regular at Brody's Pool Room. I had beaten Mr. Davis more than once playing six-ball for money. "Reggie Longcrier," he said with a big grin on his face.

"Do you know Reggie, Mr. Davis?"

"Sure, I know Reggie. Reggie's a bit of a hustler. He thinks he's slick." I then asked Mr. Davis what he was doing there.

Mr. Davenport said, "Tommy is my assistant in training."

Tommy said, "I'll bet if you make him empty his pockets, you'll find some dice and some cards. Ain't no telling what else you might find."

Davenport then said, "Reggie, empty everything out of your pockets onto my desk." As I emptied my pockets, I noticed that Tommy was getting quite a kick out of this as I pulled out a deck of cards, some dice, and a small roll of money.

Then Tommy said, "Let me pat him down."

Then Mr. Davenport said, "Stand up straight. Spread your legs and both arms out." As Tommy shook me down, he touched the bag of weed in my sock. "What's this?" he asked.

He snatched the bag of marijuana out of my sock and threw it on the desk with the rest of my belongings. "Where'd you get this?"

"I found it," I answered.

Mr. Davenport called another officer in and told him to call for a patrol car unless I told them where I got the weed. I stuck to the story that I found it. I knew that there was but so much they could do to me since I was still a teen. The patrol car took me to the station and continued questioning me about where I got the weed. They later allowed my mother to come and get me out since I was still underage. Word got out later that they had busted me for the marijuana but that I never gave up Iceman's name. When the word got to Iceman, he thanked me for not giving him up. Whenever he would see me in the pool rooms, he'd always give me a free bag of weed or some money, telling me to let him know if I ever needed anything.

Now here I was in Harlem, New York, broke, hungry, pitiful, and addicted. After standing out in front of the Shalamar for what seemed like hours, watching pimps and hustlers jumping in and out of Cadillacs talking smack, a pretty black limousine pulled to the curb and honked. It was Iceman with a big grin on his face. He waved me to get in the car. When I got in, he said, "Man, I almost didn't recognize you. You've lost a lot of weight. You messing with that scag, ain't you?" Before I could answer, he went on to say, "That stuff will make a monster out of you. You can't get no money messing with that stuff, man. That stuff ain't what it used to be. That stuff is to be sold to suckers, man. You used to be sharper than that. Now here you are in the Big Apple, trapped off like some sucker. You need to get some help and get off that mess. You can't get paid messing with that stuff." Although I was too far gone to want to hear it, I knew he was right. I was too powerless to stop. "Did you know that word on the street is that girl Cee Cee's father has a contract out on your life? They think you had something to do with her disappearance."

"No, man! That's not right!" I said. I explained to him what happened between us and when I had seen her last.

He said that he believed me. One of his girls told him that she thought Cee Cee had been with a pimp named Preacher and she had gotten away from him after a few days. Iceman said that he knew Preacher. He would check it out and get back to me in a few days. He handed me a hundred-dollar bill and told me to get off the streets. He didn't want to see me like this again. He said he would try to speak to the girl's father about lifting the contract.

I got back in my car and went to Adle's on 118th Street for a nice, home-cooked meal. After leaving Adle's with a full stomach, I stepped outside and ran into Cuda on his way into Adle's to sell some incense. He was trying to hustle up enough to get a fix. I said, "Go on in. See what you can do. Whatever you do, I'll put the rest with it. We'll go get some dope plus a little cocaine to go with it."

Once Cuda came out, we were off to the races! By midnight, I was broke again. After running half the night, the last bit of cocaine was the best we had gotten all night. Although I was broke, I wasn't ready to quit. Cuda disagreed. He said, "Let's get some rest for tonight and then hit it again in the morning."

That night, the only thing I could think of was the predicament I was in with a contract on my head and the possibility of Cee Cee not being found. *What if they find her dead?* I thought. *They would think I killed her. What if Iceman can't talk her father out of putting the contract on me? What if I'm blamed for her death? I don't even have a good alibi!* These were the thoughts racing through my head. "Cuda, how much dope do you think we can get for this diamond ring I've got?" I asked. I had gotten rid of a gold chain, a gold bracelet, and a very expensive watch within a three-month span. Ever since I left Cee Cee that night, everything seemed to be going downhill for me. Now I was trying to sell the ring that I vowed I would never sell.

Cuda said, "All we can do is take it to the man and see what he gives up for it." Five bags of heroin, five caps of coke, and about sixty bucks was the price I bargained for my ring that night. It would soon be gone within an hour.

"What if she's dead? What if they blame me? What if Iceman can't talk her father down from the contract? I'm a dead duck! Cuda, what you think I can get for this car tonight?" I asked.

He said, "Wait a minute, man! We need the car to hustle with in the morning. The car is gonna help us get some more money. You don't want to sell the car, man. Why don't you just call it a night?"

I was really out of it and said, "Well, if you don't go with me, I'll go by myself."

Cuda couldn't believe it. "Man, you're crazy! Don't nobody get rid of the car they hustle with? That's just like giving away your money!"

I answered, "Man, I don't want to hear all of that. Are you going with me or not?" That night, I sold my Cadillac Coupe for six hundred fifty dollars on a street corner in Harlem. Hours later, I was dead broke without a dime in my pocket. I looked down at both arms and the damage done trying to find the right vein to serve me in my insanity. I poked them until they were swollen with dried-up blood. I had nothing to live for, and I cursed the day I was born. As I walked out into the night from the shooting gallery, Cuda turned to me and asked where I was going. I said, "Well, I used to at least have a car to sleep in. Now I don't even have that."

"Well, you can spend the night with me," he offered. I followed Cuda to 123rd Street in the middle of the block between Seventh and Eighth. It appeared that everyone in the block had their lights off and gone to bed. I followed him as he tiptoed up a set of stairs as if he was being careful not to wake anybody up.

He opened the screen door and then another door to let himself in. He reached as if to turn on a light but grabbed a box of matches on a shelf in the hallway. He struck a match to light a nearby candle that he had picked from a shelf. As my eyes became accustomed to the light, I began to study the floors, walls, and ceiling. I realized that we were spending the night in an abandoned house and all the rest of the houses in the block were abandoned. I found out later that this was the best one in the block. This became my resting place for weeks to come as my drug problem dictated the terms of my existence.

18

MORE ADVENTURES IN NEW YORK

The whereabouts of Cee Cee haunted me for months to come, and the drugs took complete control of my life. Every waking hour was dedicated to feeding the monkey that was riding my back. I was spending a hundred fifty to three hundred dollars a day to satisfy my addiction. Heroin and cocaine were the order of the day. They held me a willing captive. I was always ready to serve, risking life and freedom for the next fix. I felt surely heroin and cocaine would follow me all the days of my life and I would dwell in the house of pain forever!

I was not in denial about my drug problem. I would admit that, but I denied that there was anything else wrong with me besides the drugs. I thought that if I could just get a handle on this drug problem, everything else would be all right. If I could just take control of my life back from my addiction, I could get another car, get my wardrobe together, get some more jewelry, and take a big sting (the takings or rewards of a crime). I heard about a drug program called ARC at the northeast corner of 128th Street and Park Avenue, and I decided to get some help before it was too late. I had signed in and got an available bed in one of their buildings on 124th Street off of Eighth Avenue. In the mornings, we would all walk from 124th Street to 132nd on the east side to the main building where we would eat breakfast and attend groups. During the day, we were allowed to work. They would take a percentage of our earnings for a savings account until we were ready to leave.

Since they never bothered to check on us, I would go out every morning and hustle throughout the day, pretending to work. Every Friday, I would give them money to put into my savings until I was ready to leave. I needed the structure, the people, and the accountability of this program to give me the discipline that I needed to stay clean, to recover, and to regroup. Some evenings I would even enjoy a good game of chess with the program director, Mr. Allen. Mr. Allen once served many years in the federal prison and had been a junkie living on the streets of Harlem. His story was well-known. He was admired and respected by city officials, clergy, street hustlers, and junkies. My problem was that I just wasn't ready yet. At twenty-seven years old, I still felt I had many more tricks and schemes in my bag that had yet to be tried. I felt that all I had to do was *just* get control of the drugs.

About a month later, I ran into a homeboy downtown named Seabrook. Seabrook and I were raised together in public housing when we were kids. He had been running with a couple of guys named Sticks and Scooby who could speak Spanish fluently, playing three-card monte in midtown Manhattan. They were very good at their game. I had been selling fake jewelry, which was a slower hustle than playing the monte game. Seabrook convinced them to bring me in to play lookout and shield. Occasionally, I tossed the cards when they would get too hot or too known by law enforcement. Although we would cut up good money on the days we played, these guys only came out three or four days a week. I would sell watches and rings on the days they didn't show up to keep a steady flow of money coming in. I now felt ready to leave the program since I had built up quite a bit of savings. I felt I needed to get a place somewhere in midtown Manhattan closer to the action. The closest place I could find that would fit my budget and pay weekly was a room at the YMCA on Thirty-Fourth Street downtown between Eighth and Ninth Avenues. Seabrook would call me at the Y most mornings to let me know they were coming in on the train from Brooklyn. We would all meet up at Nathan's on Forty-Third and Broadway.

After about six months of playing together, Sticks and his kid brother formed a monte team of their own. Scooby Doo had fallen in love and gotten married. Seabrook and I held the team together by recruiting Johnny Cool, who was out of Detroit, and Pretty Melvin out of Texas. Both were part-time pimps. Their lives were like the song lyrics, "You know it's hard out here for a pimp when trying to get this money for the rent, for the Cadillacs, and gas money spent." These guys would play with us a few days a week to build up a bank, take care of the rent for the week, and occasionally buy a new outfit until times got better. Seabrook and I would play every day even on Sunday afternoon in Central Park. Although we made lots of money every day, it seemed that we were never able to shake the insatiable appetite for drugs. I was back to doing enormous amounts of cocaine and heroin at the end of each day, leaving me just about broke before the morning came.

One night while in a shooting gallery doing some drugs, two women who had been sharing what seemed like a bag of heroin asked what line of work we were in. Seabrook looked up, beaming with pride, and said, "We're red-card players." Everybody knew that monte players made good money and were given first-class service with protection in most shooting galleries we would patronize. Many times, stick-up boys would come through asking the house man's permission for who they could stick up, but we were always given a pass because we were good for business. We sometimes spent up to a thousand dollars a night between us and paying the houseman not to let anybody else in for the night. One of the women named Sandra asked me where we played the game. I told her that we played midtown. As we continued to talk, I found out that she had been a shield for a monte team that had played in Harlem. I played in Harlem before on 125th Street, and I was somewhat familiar with her team. However, Harlem was too hard and too risky, and did not enough money to make it worth my while. It wasn't unusual for someone to come up in your game with a pistol in a paper bag in broad daylight and take all your money. As I continued to talk to Sandra that night, I learned that not only was she a shield, but she was also a solid professional pickpocket, two months pregnant, and had just gotten out of Rikers Island.

She gave me her number and said that I could call her to come downtown and shield for us. Seabrook and I discussed the possibility of her playing with us and that it might be a good idea to have a female on the team. She started coming downtown to play with us when she wasn't out with her usual team of pickpockets. About a month later, Sandra and I got a place at the Opera Hotel around Seventy-Sixth and Broadway. Some days when my team didn't feel like working, I would bring Sandra downtown to work with me and hired two lookouts to watch for the police. This seemed to work out fine because I didn't have to cut up the money with anybody else, I would just pay my lookouts. Whenever I would play with Seabrook and my regular team, I would have to send Sandra with another team because they didn't like the idea of having to pay Sandra and me both. Other teams were glad to pay her because she was worth it. She knew how to toss the cards almost as good as some of the others. As the months went by, I got arrested almost every other week for playing three-card monte on the streets. Most of the detectives that worked the Midtown South Precinct knew me on a first-name basis, even knowing most of the alias I had used.

During Sandra's eighth and ninth month of pregnancy, I kept her playing with me most days. One day in her ninth month, we were playing downtown on Delancey Street. It was on a Saturday afternoon, and I had already been given one warning by the officer that worked that beat. Even so, I wasn't ready to leave since I hadn't made my quota for the day. Once the officer was out of sight, I set up again. This guy had given me a good warning and told me his supervisor was putting pressure on him to lock up all monte players that day. Instead of taking the warning and moving my game somewhere else, I disregarded and disrespected this officer by playing anyway. I was tossing the cards with a large crowd flowing from the sidewalk to the street. "Who'll give me fifty? Who'll give me a hundred? Fifty will get you a hundred, a hundred will get you two hundred." Soon my lookouts were breaking the game up and ushering me out of the crowd. "Get up! The officer is coming back up the street!" They took the cards out of my hand.

Sandra went in the opposite direction, knowing to meet me around the corner in the restaurant where we had planned to meet if we got separated. After waiting awhile for Sandra in the restaurant, another monte player from another team came in and said that the officer had arrested Sandra and one of his team. The officer told her that since he couldn't catch me, he was going to take her to jail. She was nine-months pregnant! To make matters worse, she had pending charges and quite an extensive criminal record. It was Saturday evening, and I wondered if she could get on the court docket for Sunday since court closed at six that day. That night, I contacted an attorney who said that he would try and pull her if he could get her before the judge on Sunday. That Sunday, the lawyer was able to get her cut loose because she was nine-months pregnant. The judge gave her some mercy in spite of her pending charges. I believe that the good Lord knew that this girl needed a break, and she needed it then.

The next morning after she got out, her water broke. My homey Hippo just came over that morning to see if I would give him some work. The next thing I knew, Sandra was on her knees, holding on to the edge of the bed and hollering. "I think I'm gonna have it now! I think I'm gone have it now!" she screamed. I told Hippo to go to the desk downstairs and tell them to call an ambulance. She was getting ready to have this baby! Minutes later, Hippo returned saying that the ambulance was on its way. He told me they said if she had the baby before they got there to have her lie on her back and put the baby on her chest. In the meantime, Sandra continued to holler louder on her knees. "I believe it's coming! I believe it's coming! I believe it's coming!" I pleaded with her to wait until the ambulance got there because I didn't know any better. She started hollering louder, "It's coming! It's coming! It's coming!" While still on her knees, she pushed out a small piece of humanity. We quickly put her on her back as instructed with the baby on her chest. She cried, "I hope it don't die!"

Hippo noticed that the umbilical cord was wrapped around the baby's neck so we unwrapped the cord from around the baby's neck. I asked Hippo, "Aren't we supposed to cut the cord?"

"I think so," he says. "You want to use my knife?"

I said, "Yeah, you hold this end of the cord while I cut it."

Just in the nick of time, an officer walked in the door and rushed to grab my hand. "No, you're *not* supposed to do that! You've got to wait on the ambulance to get here!"

The paramedics arrived, put clamps on each end of the umbilical cord, cut it with a razor-like object, and tied a knot. I rode with her and this newborn human to the Roosevelt Hospital. She hollered again louder than ever before as they got the afterbirth out of her. Sandra had someone come to the hospital and take the baby. I never saw it again. Weeks later, it was back to business. Some evenings when we would get through hustling cards for the day, we would hang out in the chess club up the stairs on Forty-Second Street between Eighth and Broadway. Seabrook and I would challenge one another to a game of chess hoping to curb the urge to take the number two train up to Harlem to get high. The club was always lively with chess and backgammon players playing for a quarter a point. In a large room nearby, a few Jewish rabbis and others would be indulging in a game of gin rummy.

Sometime later, Seabrook introduced me to a tall, white fellow with coal-black hair and a baby face named Bruce who made a hustle at playing backgammon. He was like the fast Eddie of the chess club. Whenever someone would come in from out of town or some other place around New York looking to play a game of backgammon for some money, the houseman would always direct them to Bruce. He sat in the same place just about all day and half the night, always ready to play anybody for any amount of money. I heard that Bruce was one of the ten best backgammon players in the world. I had always found backgammon to be a rather slow hustle, and thought that Bruce could make a lot more money with Seabrook and me if he would play the red card with us during the early part of the day. We told him we would pay him anywhere from a hundred to one-fifty dollars a day and decided to break him in on some side streets in midtown, showing him how to bet, when to bet, and what to say. Soon, Seabrook and I were cutting up a thousand to twelve thousand a day. We would pay Bruce a hundred fifty dollars a day as we promised, and he was always happy to receive it because it only took him from his office corner in the chess club for a few hours. Seabrook and I would buy a few outfits that we had our eyes on then catch a train straight to Harlem to spend the rest of the night, blowing the rest of our money on cocaine and heroin until we were broke.

The following morning, we had to depend on Bruce to buy us breakfast and furnish the bank to start the day. Each day was the same as our drug habits called for more and more. Sometimes we'd have to call Bruce in the middle of the night after we both had gotten broke and ask to borrow a hundred against the next day's take. Although we'd always straighten it out the following day, he was now asking for a bigger cut of the money we were making. I couldn't blame him since we were waking him up all hours of the night, having him to buy our breakfast in the morning, and furnishing the bank for us to play with. We were now at his mercy.

A few weeks after that, I was picked up for playing monte on Forty-Second Street and Broadway. I would spend a few months in Rikers Island because of a few failure-to-appear warrants from the past for playing monte. After I went to Rikers, Seabrook took a break from playing the game.

19

FROM RIKERS ISLAND
TO WALL STREET

My friend Bruce was glad to see me once I got out not just because of the money we made together, but he sincerely wanted to see me drug-free. He wanted me to meet Neil, another clean-cut white guy who frequently played at the chess club and knew Bruce. Bruce thought it would be good to have another white guy on the team to play with us and that we would probably make more money. We decided we would start Neil off at a hundred bucks to break him in and then we would pay him more once he learned how to shield as Bruce did. I wanted us to go to Wall Street to play because we could make money there if we had the right team.

Seabrook said, "If we get caught playing down there, they might throw us under the jail!"

I was more confident. "Not if we take two seasoned lookouts who know how to watch out for the detectives. We shouldn't have any problems especially if we don't play too long."

Seabrook asked, "Do I have to toss them?"

I said, "Of course you do. I just got out, remember?"

Usually if you just got out of jail, most teams would give you a bit of a grace period before they asked you to start throwing again. This was just a courtesy among certain teams. Most of us who played regular had anywhere from thirty to fifty arrests for playing the red card on the streets of New York. We would always much rather be a shield than to be the thrower because that's who the police would take to jail. Every now and then, they would take the whole team to jail; most of the time, they just arrested the thrower who would be back on the street in a day or two, depending on the docket for court.

Since we had decided that we would play Wall Street, I asked Bruce and Neil to wear suits and ties the next day. "If we're gonna play Wall Street, you guys got to look like you belong in Wall Street," I said.

The next day, Bruce and Neil were ready, dressed in suits and ties looking like two Wall Street executives. Between the hours of 11:00 a.m. and 2:00 p.m. the following day, we would cut up close to four thousand for the first day on Wall Street playing monte. We would play on Wall Street for months before I was given my first citation for playing the red card. All I had to do was go to court and pay a fifty or hundred fine. If I had been playing in midtown with my record, I would have been locked up. We decided we would play Wall Street until we couldn't play it anymore. When word got out that they were only giving citations for playing the red card on Wall Street, other teams began to flood it with monte games until citations became days in jail.

One day, I made good money the day before so I decided to take a break from playing and spend some money. Earlier that afternoon Sandra wanted to go do a little shopping on Thirty-Fourth Street. After we purchased several items, we walked with our bags in hand down the street, passing a few monte games with a crowd placing their bets.

Just to see what was happening, Sandra and I looked over into one of the games to see who was playing. We knew most of the teams that played in midtown along with most of the detectives. As we approached, we heard one of the lookouts warn the players that the police were coming. Sandra and I moved away, relieved that we had taken the day off. As we continued to walk with the bags, I noticed a detective who had arrested me on several occasions for playing monte in midtown. He headed toward us, looking straight ahead and not noticing us. For some reason or another, I thought that it would be nice to speak to him just to let him see I was off and that I had been shopping. I called out to him. Once I had gotten his attention, I waved at him. He turned around and came over to me saying that I had made it easy for him by not having to chase after me. He pushed me up against a building.

I said, "Wait a minute, man. I wasn't playing any cards today. I've been shopping. Here are my bags. I don't even have any cards on me."

He didn't care about that. " Don't worry, I've got plenty of cards down at the precinct." He allowed Sandra to take the bags I was carrying. She tried to convince him I wasn't playing and that we were shopping. He cuffed me and said, "Come on, let's go. I'll give you a break next time. I need the overtime." It wasn't unusual that a detective would arrest a monte player just to get some overtime, especially when they would take their time getting you on docket by not showing up the next day. Once we got to the precinct, I continued to say how wrong he was for doing this to me. He just laughed, pulled out three cards from his desk drawer, started tossing them on his desk, and asked me to try to catch his red card. He said if I caught it, he would turn me lose. Then he said, "You know, I've been practicing so that when I retire from the force, I can make as much money as you guys." He counted my money. While the other detectives wrote up the paperwork, he said, "Let Reggie keep his money. He's got six hundred dollars here." He then turned to me and said, "See there, you know I could take the money as evidence but I'll let you keep your money." He was right. If he wanted to be dirty, he could have taken my money and there would have been nothing I could have done about it.

Months later, I would be playing alongside two other monte teams at night on Forty-Fourth and Broadway. Detective Whal and Dominique, along with some other detectives, arrested the other players, leaving me and my team. They said as they hauled the others off to jail, "Reggie, that's the one we owe you."

Sandra and I later moved up to the Bronx on West Farms Road into a two-bedroom apartment. Shortly after we moved to the Bronx, Sandra introduced me to a Nigerian named Boston Blackie. He was very dark-skinned, almost five ten, and built like a linebacker. He would sip on a pint of Seagram's Seven every day. Unlike the rest of us who played monte, he played the game with three round, black disk-like leather objects. He would color one with white chalk, saying, "Find the white, the black loses. The white man wins, the black man loses."

Sandra met him and his wife while I was in Rikers Island. He saw to it that Sandra had work and money while I was gone. Boston Blackie and I became good friends and worked together for the next year. He would always be the thrower while I, his wife, and Sandra were the shield. This meant there would be less risk for me going to jail and was a far better arrangement than me throwing the cards and taking the most risk as I had done with other teams. I also got to drive home every night in his new Cadillac because he would be too drunk to drive. I would first drive him to Brooklyn and then take the car home to the Bronx. I would drive back to Brooklyn in the morning to pick him up, and we would start our day once again.

A year later while Boston Blackie was working with his partners, running an after-hours joint in Brooklyn, two stick-up men walked in with pistols, demanding money, including Boston Blackie's. One of the robbers saw the glimmer of a cluster of diamonds on a ring that Boston Blackie was wearing and demanded that he take the ring off and give it to him. Blackie refused because he had already given him a large sum of money. He just wasn't ready to part with his ring. The gunman shot him in the head and killed him for that ring. I didn't remember if there was ever a funeral service for Blackie. I guess everything was moving at such a breathless pace that no one even had time to mourn his passing.

20

DOPE FIEND

The next few months were very rough for me as my drug habit got worse and worse. I threw all caution to the wind in my pursuit to get high. One day, Johnny Cool and I had made an early hustle and decided that we would run uptown to Harlem for a couple of hours to buy some drugs. Once we got to 116th Street and Eighth Avenue, I ran into a homeboy we called Himey. He had been touting for some young dope kids on 117th Street. A *touter* was someone who would send or bring customers to the dealer and would be paid in product for his assistance.

"Hey, Reg, you looking for something?" he asked.

"Yeah, what's good out here?" I asked.

"These kids got that Blue Magic, the best dope out here. If you're gonna buy some cocaine, Black Earnie is the way to go. Plus, you can get off in my spot on 116th Street. You want me to cop for you?" he asked.

I answered, "You get the dope (heroin), and I'll see Black Earnie about the cocaine." I gave him enough money to get something for himself to help keep him honest. I would always buy enough cocaine to share with him.

Once we got to the shooting gallery, he only had two sets of works. Himey allowed Johnny and I to use them, waiting for one of us to get finished so he could do his. Once I got my shot and drew the blood into the syringe, I began to walk the floor talking about how good the coke was. Suddenly, the front door flew open and three men walked in with heavy coats buttoned up from the cold. I greeted them with the needle still in my arm. "This is some good cocaine. If you ain't got Black Earnie's cocaine, you ain't got nothing."

The pistols come out, pointing at Johnny and mine's foreheads. "Give it up and hit the floor, everybody!"

Himey pleaded with them, "Come on, y'all. Don't do this to us. We ain't got much of nothing! We're just trying to get high like y'all. Come on, you ain't got to do this to us!"

By this time, I was numbed of any emotion and feeling too good at the moment to let this interruption mess with my high so I did just as I was told. I laid on the floor with the syringe still in my arm and handed them the little money and dope I had left in my pockets. I had known better than to have more money than I could stand to lose while in the shooting gallery of Harlem. They put our coats over our heads and told us not to look. They allowed me to keep what I had left in my cooker and then suddenly left with Himey running behind them and telling them how wrong they had been for doing this to him and his friends. Actually, Himey had been a part of it all along. He set us up knowing we were used to making good money but this time, we stashed our money before coming to Harlem because we had not yet finished hustling for the day. I would always keep a small stash in the soles of my socks just in case something went wrong like this. The stick-up men left.

Himey came back into the room. He said, "I don't know why them guys would do that. I'm going after them. I'll be back."

I said, "Before you go, take this with you!" Then I kicked him as hard as I could in his groin. As he bent over, I started punching him in the head and looked around for some heavy object to hit him with.

Himey escaped my wrath, yelling, "I was not a part of it!"

In the meantime, Johnny Cool stood still in a state of shock at what had just taken place. He was not used to Harlem or what could happen in Harlem. Johnny and I went back to midtown and finished playing for the day. Later that evening, I decided to buy a brand-new Hawkbill knife and go back to Harlem to look for Himey. I just couldn't let him get away with crossing me like he did, especially since I had always treated him fairly.

For the next week or so, I would make trips to 116th Street and Eighth Ave, walking around a four or five block radius looking for Himey. For some reason, I could not rest until I hurt him. About a month later, I got word that Himey had been killed in Harlem. I heard that two dope boys came to one of the shooting galleries one morning to give out samples of heroin as they would often do from time to time. Word on the street was that Himey had taken the deadbolt off the door so that the stick-up boys could come in and rob them. Once the kids found out that Himey had set them up, they put a contract on his life and had him killed.

The places that I had been buying my drugs in Harlem were becoming more and more dangerous. At the rate I was going, I figured it would be just a matter of time before something would happen to me. I started bypassing Harlem and bought my drugs in Bronx closer to where I lived, as if that would lessen the danger of what I was doing. I was still playing a dangerous game of Russian roulette with my life. One evening after having a good day of hustling with my cut being seven or eight hundred dollars, I decided I would buy a few new outfits and a new portable TV before going to the Bronx. I brought the TV from one of the stores on Forty-Second Street. Sandra hailed a cab to take us to the Bronx. First, I bought some drugs with Sandra holding the cab around the corner from where the drugs were being sold. I then got back in the cab, and we went to our small apartment. After making several trips back and forth buying more drugs, I was just about broke. I decided I would take the TV that I had just bought back to the store. I reasoned that I would get my money back, buy some more drugs, and get another TV tomorrow. I gathered my receipt, instructions, the TV, and caught the subway back downtown to Forty-Second Street about ten thirty, hoping that the store did not close yet since most of the stores that sold this kind of stuff remained open long after the other stores.

I rushed toward the store. I saw the lights were still on, the gates had not gone down, and people were still moving around. I breathed a sigh of relief. Once in the store, I motioned for the salesman who sold me the TV. "Man, I need to get my money back from this TV I bought earlier from you." He told me that the store policy was that they would trade it for another one. I thought, *This is not working as I had planned. I can't go back uptown to the Bronx empty-handed after all this hassle.* I didn't even have a train fare to get back. I turned to the salesman and said, "Look, man, let's work something out here. Why don't you let me buy one of these little radios here in exchange for the TV and give me back the difference in money?"

"I'm sorry. I can't do that either," he said.

Determined not to leave empty-handed, we decided on an offer he couldn't refuse. I offered to give the TV for only half the money back with the understanding that if I came back within twenty-four hours with the other half, he would give me the TV back. If not, I would be the loser. Although

I knew I would not come back for the TV, I reasoned that I had made a pretty good bargain, trying to convince myself that I was not completely crazy. Once back uptown at the Bronx, I decided to cop my dope from some Hispanics who were selling out of a building around the corner from where I lived. These guys would sell their drugs from the third floor hallway of the building with *touters* and lookouts at the bottom of the stairs.

As I walked in the building, I walked passed this young kid who was always on point whenever I came. He was one of the lookouts who would control the traffic in and out of the building. He couldn't have been more than sixteen years old. He would be at the bottom floor, allowing one to go up and cop while another would come back down. As I passed him, I greeted him as always with a handshake and a smile, asking if anyone was upstairs and was the dope still good. He was always glad to see me because I would give him a five dollar bill for himself. He motioned for me to go on up, and that everything was all right. Once I got to the third landing, I had the feeling that something was amiss. Usually, there were always three guys on the floor selling. One that had the dope, one that took the money, and one would be holding the gun protecting the business. This time, there was only one man to greet me.

I asked, "What's happening?" Suddenly, he pulled a knife from his pocket and began to stab wildly at me. I was able to get a few punches off, hitting him in his nose and his mouth and finally grabbing the hand that had the knife. I twisted it until he dropped it on the floor. I saw the young kid coming up the stairs after hearing the commotion. I said to him as he approached the landing, "This guy tried to stick me up!"

By this time, I had his head locked in my arms. The young kid picked up the knife and motioned with it to turn the man loose. I realized then that they had been together and it had been a setup. The guys who had been selling on the third floor were gone for the night. These guys were planning to rob anybody who came to cop some drugs. A feisty young woman came out of her apartment to protest the disturbance in her building. She realized what was happening and told these two guys she wanted them out of her building or she would call the police. The guy I had in the headlock was telling the kid to stick me with the knife. I could see from the expression on the kid's face that he had not expected things to turnout the way they did as he could see his friend in the headlock with blood coming from both his nose and mouth. A couple more people came out of their apartments on that floor. All of them were telling these guys that they wanted them out of their building.

Seeing the frightened kid holding the knife, I gradually loosed my grip on the man's neck and pushed him down the steps with the kid grabbing hold of him. The man said, "I'm gonna kill you when you come out!"

The feisty woman grabbed my arm and whispered, "Don't go back down that way. Go to the roof and cross over to the next building."

I did just as she had said, going to the roof of the building and crossed over to the next roof, which happened to be my building. I came down and went into our apartment. I told Sandra what had happened as I wiped the blood off of my leather jacket, seeing knife slits where the man tried to stab me. About 30 minutes later, we heard an ambulance and sirens. We could look over to the next building entrance from our bedroom window. We saw the paramedics bringing someone out on a stretcher. We both wondered what happened. The next day, we learned that the same guy who attempted to rob me had stabbed and killed the next guy that came in after me. They said that he was stabbed viscously multiple times. Looking back, that could have been me.

Weeks later, I was in Harlem again looking for my homeboy Fat Back. I heard that he was dealing a good package and was looking out for the homeboys coming through to buy dope. I first ran into his women on 126th Street and Eighth Ave. Chicky was his woman and had been strung out on heroin since she was a kid. Sometimes she'd get high and sing on the corner while crowds would gather to listen. I heard that she sang in a competition at the Apollo Theater as a kid and lost to a twelve-year-old blind boy named Stevie Wonder. She had never been right since. She was resigned to be a heroin addict until she died.

"Hey, Chicky, where is Fat Back?" I asked.

"He's over on 127th Street. Come on, I'll take you to him. Fatback was just talking about you just the other day. He'll be glad to see you!" she answered.

As we approached 127th Street, we saw a crowd gathered in the middle of the street around a car accident. Someone had been hit crossing the street. The man who was hit laid in the street, waiting for someone to help him. Another man with a bat began to beat him repeatedly, saying, "I told you I'd get you back, didn't I? I told you I'd get you back!" The man with the bat was my friend Fatback.

I found out that the fellow who had been hit by the car, the one that Fatback was beating, was a guy Fat Back fought with over some drugs two weeks before. Now Fatback had seized the opportunity to finish the fight. He turned quickly and disappeared into the crowd. Chicky and I caught up with him minutes later.

"Man, what did that guy do that made you beat him after he'd been hit by a car?" I asked. He grinned and explained what had gone down. He couldn't resist the opportunity to see him on his back in the street.

My drug addiction continued to get worse and worse. I was a spiraling, out-of-control addict and was losing my relationship with Sandra. By this time, we had just about gotten on each other's last nerve. We were no good for each other but neither one of us wanted to be the first to say goodbye. One night, I blew my whole bank roll sitting in a shooting gallery in Harlem, mainlining a mixture of heroin and cocaine into my veins all night until both arms were swollen and sore. I decided to buy a quarter pint of five-star brandy from the liquor store to level me off. While in the liquor store, I ran into a hustler named Clean out of Savannah, Georgia.

"Hey, Reg, what you up to?" he asked.

"Ain't nothing, man. I just bought me a quarter pint of Brandy to level me off and call it a night. Why? What's up? You doing something?" I asked.

"Yeah, I'm on my way to North Carolina to pick up my woman." She's got a doctor there and she gets these Dilaudids from him. "Why don't you ride with me to keep me company? We can hustle our way down and back doing a little shortchanging and selling some jewelry I've got in the trunk," he offered.

I wasn't much interested in the Dilaudids but the jewelry was right up my alley. I felt if I didn't get out of New York now while I had the chance, I'd never leave New York. I gulped down the small bottle of Brandy I had in a paper bag and said "Let's go!" He offered to take me by my spot to get my clothes, but I said, "No, man, this is it. I'm leaving with what I got on my back. I'll buy me some new stuff on the road. If I'm gonna leave New York, I've got to leave now."

"What about Sandra?" he asked.

"Sandra will have to take care of herself. I'm outta here," I answered.

21

DOWN SOUTH

Clean and I left New York that night about one in the morning, heading for North Carolina. By the time we arrived in Charlotte the next day, I hustled up enough money to buy a couple of new outfits along with some shoes and underwear. After a few days, Clean and his woman were ready to head back to New York. I decided I would stay in the south to finish kicking my habit and get back on my feet. I hooked up with a team of slum hustlers out of Charlotte who had transportation and were pretty fond of me. These guys looked after me and nurtured me back to health. They had been strictly about their business and would only drink in moderation. Although I had some kinsfolk living in Hickory, I did not want them to see me until I had gotten on my feet. That didn't take very long.

Within a few months, I was able to purchase a forest-green Oldsmobile '98. I was ready to move to Hickory, see some kin folk, and settle in. Once in Hickory, I found my way to the gambling spots and was hustling three-card monte in the pool rooms. I earned quite a reputation with the cards so everybody started calling me "Three-Card."

My friends from Charlotte and I were on the road Thursday through Saturday, hustling fake jewelry throughout North Carolina. We would get back to Hickory on Saturday evening in time to go to a gambling spot. Sometimes we just went to a club to drink and dance for a little fun. This was a lot better than blowing hundreds of dollars a night in some shooting gallery in New York. I was feeling better than I felt in a long time. I had money, clothes, jewelry, and a car. It was Super Bowl season and the big game was in Miami. Most hustlers worth their salt would be headed that way. My friend Oscar from Charlotte wanted to order a load of watches, rings, and bracelets to take down to Miami. We usually ordered our pieces from a place in Washington D.C. and had them shipped one day in advance COD to a post office wherever we were going. This time, we had our shipment sent to Atlanta so we could work there for a week before heading to Miami. It seemed like every pimp, hustler, and con man from all over had the same idea because Atlanta was the last watering hole for hustlers on the way to Miami. All of the spots most frequented by hustlers such as the San Suzie on West Peachtree, the Silver Fox Lounge on Camelton Road, and Billy's in Buckhead were packed every night. The ladies of the night would pack Peachtree Street. In almost all of the nightspots, the restrooms would be filled with people passing samples of cocaine around in a ten-dollar bill as a friendly gesture. I would take great pride in saying, "No, thank you. I don't mess with that stuff no more," but I was still drinking Remy Martin every night. My lifestyle had not changed.

Weeks after the Super Bowl, I was back in Atlanta and bought another car, a brand-new Ford LTD. My friend Oscar was getting homesick and missed his girlfriend back in Charlotte so I let him take my Oldsmobile back while I remained in Atlanta. Later, I moved to Decatur with my girlfriend who was known by everyone as "Doll." Doll worked as a dancer in one of the bars on Peachtree Street. She had a gift for turning a Timex into a Rolex with rubbing alcohol, toothpicks, and some stencil. She was paid handsomely for her skills. Doll became a great asset to me. In February, I went to Charlotte to check on Oscar who still had my other car. I wanted to convince him to go with me to Mardi Gras in New Orleans to do some work. He had never been before. I was used to going every year from New York with a monte team and making lots of money. I wasn't able to convince him to go because he didn't want to leave his woman for that long. I had really planned on going that year but I didn't want to go by myself.

One morning, Oscar and I had just finished eating breakfast at one of the restaurants on Trade Street in Charlotte up from the Trailways bus station. As we were getting into the car, I looked up the street and I saw four men walking toward us coming from the direction of the bus station. Two of the men looked familiar as they got closer. I recognized them as monte card players I worked with on the streets in New York. Greg was a tall, slender, dark-skinned guy who wore black-rimmed glasses. He was with an older Hispanic gentleman. The other two men were the old man's sons. They were riding the bus from New York to Mardi Gras, playing three-card monte on the way. The driver told them several times to stop but since they didn't, they were put off the bus.

I was glad to see them and they were certainly glad to see me. They had not expected to see anyone they knew in Charlotte. After they told me what had happened on the bus, I offered to take them to New Orleans if they would pay for the gas. They were more than glad to do so. I got everyone in the car with the few bags they were carrying. I told Oscar to take good care of my Oldsmobile and I would see him when I got back from New Orleans. I drove to my hotel room, got my few belongings checked out, and hit the road. We got to

New Orleans late that night and went straight to the French Quarter to meet up with some other teams. Word was that everybody was staying at a hotel called the Top of the Trop. Other players who arrived earlier knew we were on our way and asked the hotel manager to keep some rooms reserved for other monte players coming in from New York. They had a room reserved for me at the Top of the Trop for fifty five dollars a night, which wasn't bad for Mardi Gras season. The hotel had a soul food restaurant downstairs so everyone headed to the hotel, meeting in the restaurant to plan the following day's strategy and get a bite to eat. This was the year that the New Orleans police were supposedly going on strike. Once we had arrived at the hotel and I entered the small lobby, I knew that my stay there would be short-lived. I decided I would only pay for one night and be looking for some place else to stay the following day.

Gary and Q, who had been riding with me, both had the same idea. This wasn't quite what we expected. Our rooms were on the sixth floor. When we got off the elevator, we saw junkies going in and out of the rooms. The doors were ajar. They were cooking their heroin while sitting or standing with needles in their arms, and prostitutes brought their johns up and down the stairwell. When we met in the restaurant downstairs, I placed my order for red beans and rice. I expressed my feelings about staying in this hotel given the current environment especially since I wasn't shooting heroin anymore. The following morning, quite a few of us checked out to look for another hotel while others were content to stay where they were. All of the hotels in New Orleans were full, and people were renting out rooms in their homes. Even beauty shops and barber shops were renting sleeping space for would-be squatters.

Gary, Q, his two sons, and I found a hotel in Jefferson Parish, which was about eight or nine miles outside New

Orleans. It wasn't even a three-star hotel but it was much better than what we had before. That afternoon, we settled into our rooms and went back to New Orleans. We headed straight to the French Quarter. I remember thinking how sweet it was gonna be because the police were on strike. They would be short with manpower so we all figured they would be too preoccupied with the heavier stuff and pay little attention to monte players. As we approached the corner of Royal and Conti, we noticed two or three monte teams playing next to a jewelry store. We set up between the two teams. As soon as we were ready, the crowd gathered like bees around honey. This was a monte player's dream! The police were on strike, and there was nobody to hassle us except for a little old woman who owned the jewelry store. She would come out every now and then saying that the crowd was blocking her doorway and people couldn't get a good look in her window. She threatened to call the cops but nobody paid her any attention. The games continued. We figured the police were probably preoccupied in frying much bigger fish than us.

At the end of the day, every team made money. Most teams made several thousand dollars. Some called it a wrap for the day and went to the hotel to freshen up for the evening in anticipation of having fun visiting some of the night clubs around New Orleans. Myself and a few others took a break to get something to eat and kept playing throughout the night. By the time I got in that night, I made so much money I was afraid to keep it myself so I managed to get the hotel manager to keep some of it in his safe for me. That turned out to be a very wise decision. The next day, we went back to the French Quarter to set up in the same place only to find two other teams playing in front of the jewelry store. We decided we would wait awhile before setting up and just watch the other teams play.

After a few minutes, someone shouted from the other team, "The cops are coming!"

As the teams picked up their cards and disappeared into the crowd, the woman who owned the jewelry store was pushing her way through the crowd followed by two policemen. "There they are, officer. That's them! They were playing!" She pointed a boney finger at Gary, myself, and a Hispanic woman who was playing with the other team.

One officer grabbed Gary and I while the other one got the woman. Gary and I protested that we weren't playing while all the Hispanic woman could say was "I no speak English."

Our protesting and complaining fell on deaf ears. They handcuffed the three of us and threw us into the back of a police cruiser. We went straight to jail. Once we had gotten to the police station, they searched us, taking all of our money along with my driver's license. The police told us that we probably wouldn't get to court until after Mardi Gras because they had a lot of cases backed up on the docket. However, two days later, they were calling Gary and me out for court. Once we got into the courtroom, we saw old man Q sitting with his two sons and an attorney he found to represent us. We ended up getting our cases dismissed and paying court costs.

When we got our possessions back, I noticed that my driver's license and the money I had (a little more than five hundred dollars) was not in my envelope although I had a receipt for everything they had taken when I was arrested. I questioned one of the officers about it, and he said that I would have to get in touch with the officer that arrested me. He pointed to the officer's name at the bottom of my receipt. "This officer works out of the Rampart station. You'll have to go over there."

Once I got out, I went back to the hotel to take a shower, change clothes, and get something to eat before heading to the Rampart station. The station seemed deserted when I walked in. It seemed as if they had seven officers for the whole station. I noticed a young black officer typing something on a typewriter. I said, "Say, brother, is Officer O'Reilly around here anywhere? He arrested me a few days ago. My case was heard and dismissed today but he still has some things that belong to me."

The officer on duty answered, "He's not here right now. He's on the street. Let me call him for you." Once he located the officer and told him I was there, he handed me the phone to talk with him.

I told him I was one of the fellows he had arrested recently for supposedly playing three-card monte. "My case was heard today, sir, and was dismissed. I'm here to get my driver's license and money that you took when I was arrested."

I was not ready for what I heard next. The officer said, "How could they dismiss your case without me being there? If I catch you anywhere in New Orleans tonight or any other time, I'm locking you up!"

"But, sir, I have a receipt for the amount of money you took from me. My case has been dismissed. I paid the court costs and, furthermore, I'm going to need my driver's license," I pleaded.

He was cold as ice. "You can't get no money back because I'm going to use that money as evidence to lock you back up. If you want your money and driver's license back, meet me in the French Quarter this evening so you can be my first arrest for the evening. I'll also be arresting you for driving without your license!"

Once I hung up the phone, I turned to the young officer who was typing. I pleaded my case, telling him all that Officer O'Reilly said to me. The young officer looked up from his typewriter for the first time with a sympathetic look on his face. He said, "Sorry, brother, but I can't do anything about it. This is Mardi Gras season. You ought to know that anything goes."

I knew then I was going to have to leave New Orleans that night and that I couldn't waste any time in doing it. I left the Rampart police station and headed to the hotel to pack my belongings. I let others know that I couldn't take a chance on staying with this crazy officer on the loose. It was some consolation to know I still had a stash of money in the hotel safe.

That night, I left New Orleans in a torrent of rain. While going from Louisiana into Mississippi, I noticed that my gas tank was just about empty. I approached a green metal sign that said, "Welcome to Mississippi." Next to it was a huge wooden sign in big, bold, black letters saying, "HOME OF THE KKK." As I drove further, I saw a speed limit sign that said "35." Beneath it, someone wrote "NIGGERS 100." I remember thinking that this would be the wrong place to run out of gas.

The rain was still coming down pretty hard. I didn't know God then like I know him now, but I prayed to the only god I knew at the time, the hustler's god. I asked him to protect me from any unforeseen danger and not let me run out of gas before I found a gas station. These types of prayers or rituals were not unusual among hustlers. Most of the people I knew had some kind of idol or god that they would call on in times of trouble. The pimps would call on the pimp god to send them a good prostitute who could make lots of money. Those who hustled dice and cards would call on the gambling god to ask that they would not get caught cheating. The thieves asked the larceny god to allow them to get away with what they had stolen. The confidence man would call on his con god to send him a sucker.

As I drove further up the road, I found a convenience store that had two gas pumps. The rain was coming down so hard it seemed that my windshield would break. I got out of the car and ran into the store to pay for my gas with my coat over my head to keep from getting drenched. I pumped my gas, drove off into the night, and didn't stop until I got to Atlanta. It was good that it was late and that the rain had poured down so hard. It kept people off the street while I went through the town so fast I was hardly noticed.

When I got back into Atlanta, I figured I would camp out at Doll's apartment for a few days. She was always glad to see me and she just liked having me around for conversation. After a few days, she told me about a fair at the park. She wanted us to go, take in the scenery, and maybe get a bite to eat since she was taking the rest of the day off. I agreed to go with her to the park that day. As we walked around, I noticed the crowd that came out to enjoy the day with their families and friends. It seemed like every booth or stand had a crowd around it. While Doll was trying to make up her mind about which style of earrings she liked best at one of the stands, I was trying to make up my mind where I would set up a monte game.

I found a spot next to a booth nearby and quickly set up two boxes. I began to toss the cards and do my thing. "Watch 'em and chase 'em, see where I place 'em. The red will set you ahead and the black will set you back. Who can find my red card? Ten will get you twenty and twenty will get you forty." A crowd gathered quickly. They were watchers, not betters. I continued to entice them to place their bets as I flashed a bank roll covered with a hundred-dollar bill.

Suddenly, Doll appeared from the crowd and said, "Mister, you mean to tell me that if I pick the red card for twenty dollars, you'll give me forty back?"

"That's right. Fifty will get you a hundred, and hundred will get you two hundred," I answered.

Then a man stepped forward with his son who looked to be about nine or ten years old, saying, "Hold them cards right there. I'll bet a hundred on that card there." He pointed to the card he wanted as he pulled a hundred-dollar bill from his wallet. He put it in my hand.

I asked if anybody else wanted to place a bet. When no one answered, I said, "Turn your card over, sir. *Whoops!* That's black, you lose." The man just stared in disbelief while I continued to toss the cards ("Watch 'em and chase 'em, see where I place 'em."). The man and his son disappeared from the crowd.

Minutes later, I looked up and saw an officer on a horse headed in my direction through the crowd. I stopped playing and put the cards in my pocket. I wasn't really sure whether he was coming for me or not but didn't want to take any chances. I started walking in the opposite direction. I felt someone's hand on my shoulder. When I turned to see who it was, I saw a badge flashing in my face. Behind it was the man who lost the hundred dollars saying that I was under arrest for playing cards in the park. When the officer on the horse got to us, the man explained to him that he observed me taking people's money with this card game. He was an off-duty police officer out for a day with his son. He told the officer on the horse he would be willing to make the arrest. If he would call for a patrol car to take me to head-quarters, he would come down and do all the paperwork even though he was supposed to be off. He never bothered to tell the other officer that he lost money in my game nor did he bothered to get it back. I guess he was just content in locking me up.

After spending close to three weeks in the Jefferson Street jail in Atlanta, I was released. I decided I would order a shipment of watches and rings for shipment to Charlotte and work that area for a while. Doll joined up with me weeks later after she got her affairs in order. During the day, I sold fake watches, rings, and gold bracelets. By night, I played cards and craps when I wasn't hanging out at the money changer on Statesville Avenue. Doll made new friends fast. Soon she met Reese who was a prostitute living and turning most of her dates out of a brothel on Ninth Street. One night, Doll and I had gone to see Parliament-Funkadelic and Diana Ross at the Coliseum. We sat in the money changer talking about heading toward Fayetteville since it would soon be the first of the month when the soldiers got paid.

Reese overheard our discussion and asked could she come along with us because she thought this would be a good opportunity to leave her pimp. She assured us she would carry her load. We didn't waste any time that night. The three of us struggled to get her trunk, containing her clothing and other belongings, down the back steps of the brothel. After loading the car, we headed off into the night to Fayetteville. Once we had arrived, we checked into the Prince Charles Hotel. Adjacent from the lobby of the hotel was a bar that served drinks, about three or four regulation-sized pool tables, and plenty of gambling action.

This was an atmosphere that attracted many kinds of hustlers, especially on the fifteenth and the thirtieth of the month. We spent a few weeks in Fayetteville before being run out of town by a detective who didn't like hustlers. He made an announcement in the bar one night after unplugging the jukebox. He said he was giving everybody who didn't live in Fayetteville until sundown the next day to get out of town. We didn't waste much time leaving. The next morning, we left for Norfolk, Virginia. We ended up staying on the outskirts of Norfolk in a suite on the beach with an ocean view. I teamed up with two hustlers named Sunshine and Slick I knew in New York years ago. Norfolk was their home. It was not unusual for hustlers to retreat back home to regroup after living a fast, hard-knock life in New York. Even though Sunshine and Slick had left the Big Apple, they did not leave the drugs.

Most days after we were through hustling, I would end up driving them over to Portsmouth so that they could cop from some young boys who were selling peewee caps of cocaine. Sunshine would ask if I was going to get anything while we were on our way. "Naw, man, I ain't used in almost five years now," I said with pride.

He said, "I admire and respect you for that, but don't you know that it takes at least ten years to kick a drug habit?" At the time, I looked at him like he was crazy. I thought he was just a jealous old man who missed his time of recovery. Years later, I saw that he may have been telling the truth.

In the meantime I stayed clean and stacked my money while Sunshine and Slick stayed broke using drugs. They would borrow money from me against the next day's hustle to go buy more. In reality, they were hustling me just like they hustled the marks we played every day. This seemed like déjà vu because it was the same thing Seabrook and I had done to Bruce while we were strung out years before in New York. Now life was giving me a taste of what Bruce had gone through with Seabrook and me. I realized I was going to have to cut Slick and Sunshine loose just as Bruce had to cut Seabrook and I loose.

One evening, I dropped Slick and Sunshine off in Norfolk. I decided to get some Chinese food on the way in for Doll and Reese before they went out for the night. About an hour after we finished eating, there was a loud knock on the door. I opened the door and saw two detectives were flashing badges. "Is your name Reggie Longcrier?"

"Yes, sir. What's the problem, officer?" I answered.

"You're under arrest for maintaining and frequenting a disorderly house." The officer turned to Doll and Reese. "Both of you are under arrest for frequenting a disorderly house."

They handcuffed us, did a quick search of our apartment, and took us straight to Norfolk City Jail. We weren't worried since the charges were rather meatball and we had money to make bail. I used my one phone call to call Sunshine and asked him to get us a bondsman down to the jail as soon as he could. Before they could book us, Sunshine was there, Johnny-on-the-spot, with a bondsman. One of the detectives came back to the cell block where they were holding me with about eight other guys. He said that the bondsman was there to bail me out but he would have to run a check on my name first.

Doll and Reese were being held in another section of the jail. I had to get them out also. About twenty minutes later, the detective came back to the cell block and asked me, "Have you ever been to New Jersey prison before?"

"No, sir, why?" I lied.

"You mean you've never done time in prison in New Jersey before?" he asked.

"Why, no, sir." I lied again. I thought I would get away with it because I was using a North Carolina driver's license.

The officer went on. "Well, this seems mighty strange. When we ran your name, it came back that you had violated your parole from New Jersey. I'm sorry, but we've got to put a detainer on you. We have to hold you for New Jersey to come get you in a couple days. When you go to court, you can ask to fight extradition back to New Jersey."

I knew at that moment that I had no chance of getting out. I jumped parole and crisscrossed the country for five years thinking I would never get caught. Every criminal is foolish enough to think they will never get caught. Murphy's Law says that if anything can go wrong, it will.

22

BACK UP NORTH

Now it was time for me to go back and face the music because I decided I would not fight the extradition back to New Jersey. I was on my best behavior to Reese and Doll by getting them both out on bond. I left the keys to my car with Sunshine. He promised me he would take care of it until I got out. Within ten days, I was extradited back to the New Jersey State Prison on parole violations. Several months later, I had a parole hearing and I sat before the commission to see what my fate would be.

One of the commissioners looked at my records with all of the arrests I had in New York, New Orleans, Virginia, and other places I had been. This included some aliases I used over the five years since I violated my parole. He looked up at me from the pile of papers he had in front of him, wiped his brow and said, "*Whew!* You have traveled one long rocky road." Then he sent me back to prison.

Doll went back to Atlanta. While serving my time on the parole violation, I got a letter from Reese saying she was in prison for killing a John with an ice pick for trying to take his money back from her.

To my surprise, the parole commissioner released me. I was back on the streets within six months. They did not feel sorry for me, but I guess, judging from my past record, they figured it wouldn't be long before I would be back in prison on new charges. Once I was out again, I had to get a job because this was one of the conditions of my parole. Six months in prison was not enough time for me to kick the addiction to the lifestyle I was accustomed to. It was ingrained into every fiber of my being. I had to come up with an angle to meet the conditions of my parole and satisfy my hunger for the lifestyle so I got a job driving a taxi from early evening into the wee hours of the morning. This gave me the transportation I needed to get to the action I wanted to get back on my feet. I made it known to the bartenders in all of the night spots with lots of action that if anybody needed a cab, they should call the station and ask for my cab. I made pickups to and from the casino. This lasted well into the night. The drug dealers would move large quantities of drugs from one place to another through my cab. Prostitutes would call to be picked up after robbing a John. Most street people would call my cab because they knew I could be trusted.

I made most of my money from the street hustlers. One night, a young safecracker named Levi called me to pick him up at a location on the outskirts of town. He was the youngest safecracker I knew. Levi would hit the jackpot every few months and bragged to make sure everybody else knew that he hit it big. This was the first time I saw him since I had been home. As soon as I pulled up, he ran from a doorway and jumped into my cab and said, "Hey, Reg! You made good time. I'm not going to go back to Atlantic City because I just made a nice score. I want you to take me to Philadelphia. Don't worry because I'm going to make it worth your while. I want to give you something extra to help you get back on your feet since I didn't get a chance to see you when you first came home. You know we've got to look out for one another. We go way back." When we got on the expressway headed to Philadelphia, Levi and I made light conversation about old times until he fell asleep in the back seat of my cab. Once we got to Philly, Levi handed me three stacks of money amounting to a bit more than three thousand dollars. "Here, man, take this and get back on your feet. I'll see you when I see you," he said. Today, Levi became a substance-abuse counselor in Philadelphia for many years and is married with children and grandchildren.

I took the money Levi gave me and bought plenty of cocaine to sell on the streets. It wasn't long before word got around that I had a good cocaine package. All you had to do was call my cab, and I would bring you the product as long as you were willing to pay the fare for the cab. As my cab business picked up, I had to put workers on the street to sell my product during the early hours of the day until I came on in the evening to drive my cab until seven in the morning. At this time, things were going well for me. The cab became a good cover for my operation.

One night, I got a call to pick up a rider on South Carolina Avenue. It was Stacey and her sister V. Stacey and I were good friends in the past when she worked as a police dispatcher at city hall. She always kept me informed about what was happening. Stacey was a very attractive woman. She always dressed like a model and wore some of the most beautiful hats I've ever seen. Her hats reminded me of the kind Faye Dunaway wore in the movie *The Getaway*. In addition to wearing high-dollar hats, she wore high-end shoes, suits, shirts, and sweaters. She was a high-class professional thief who stole and sold men's clothing, women's clothing, and some mink. When she saw me, she said, "Hey, Reg! What are you doing driving a cab?"

I said, "I haven't been out of the joint long. I had to figure out how to keep the parole officer off my back while staying with the action and hustling at the same time. This is how I do it."

We exchanged numbers and soon started dating. Eventually, we moved in together as my operation expanded with her invaluable help.

It was nearing time for me to get off parole. I needed to go to Norfolk to get my car from Sunshine. When I called him, he told me that he had just gotten the car tuned up and put four new tires on it. If I came to get the car now, he and Slick wouldn't have any transportation for hustling. I assured him that I would make things right for them once I had got to Norfolk. I would be there in a day or two. Two days later, I flew out of Philly to Norfolk and caught a cab to Sunshine's two-bedroom apartment where he lived with his girlfriend P.D. Sunshine was many years her senior and old enough to be her father. He had a youthful spirit and a gift of gab that could mesmerize the Virgin Mary. P.D. was a very dark-skinned woman with a muscular build, a bad temper, and was quick to fight. When I came into their apartment, I heard a baby crying.

P.D. said, "Reggie, you know I had a baby since you've been gone. He's only a couple months old."

"What's his name?" I asked.

Sunshine said, "His name is Miracle. Anytime a man my age can make a baby, it's got to be a miracle. Yeah, that's right. I named him Miracle." Sunshine had to be at least seventy-five and P.D. was only thirty-eight at the time. That baby *was* a miracle!

I reached into my bag and gave Sunshine several bags of heroin along with some cocaine. I also brought enough to sell for the couple of days that I would be there. After he and P.D. shared what I had brought them, we sat at the kitchen table, packing the drugs for sale. Sunshine took several samples to distribute on Church Street so people would know they could come see him if they wanted to by some. Soon, word was out that dope was available at Sunshine's house. All through the night, junkies came to buy. He convinced most of them to do it right there in his place. His rationale was that he didn't want anybody leaving with the drugs and possibly getting busted. He didn't want to bring the cops to his place. By the next day, I was sold out, ready to take my car and head back to Atlantic City. I left Sunshine fifteen hundred dollars, which was more than enough for him to get a *work car* as we called them.

Once back in Atlantic City, the two workers I had selling my product while I was in Norfolk sold out and were holding money for me. They were waiting for more to continue serving their customers. I supplied them with cocaine to sell, and, eventually, supplied them with heroin to sell in the months ahead. Stacey and I moved to an apartment on Atlantic Avenue, which was two blocks from the boardwalk and one block from Kentucky Avenue or "KY" as it was called. The infamous Club Harlem was on KY, along with other favorite night spots that stayed open twenty-four hours a day. The action was there so I would hang out from midnight until daybreak, as did many other hustlers.

I never considered myself a drug dealer. I was a hustler that hustled drugs amongst other hustles as a means to an end. When I felt that I was getting too hot, my name was ringing a little too loud, or someone would tell me that the police were out to get me, I would stop and began working another hustle like craps, cards, pool, or petty cons. Sometimes I would leave town to do it. After five years of living clean, I began sampling my own product and consumed large amounts of heroin and cocaine every night. I would make sure that my two workers, Buckey and Do Drop, would have enough to sell during the day. I would pick it up once I came out around midnight and mix business with pleasure up until the wee hours of the morning. This was the time I came alive and the only time that anybody would see me. Every Sunday morning at six, there would be a breakfast show at the Club Harlem. I always had a reserved table at ringside, close to the stage. As soon as I sat down, I would have a bottle of Piper's champagne brought to my table. Many thought I was at the height of my game, but I knew better because my drug habit continued to escalate night after night. I dressed sharply and looked the part, but the drugs had begun to take their toll on me.

At this time, secret committees of the nightlife were planning to crown me "king of the nightlife." This was a coveted award among hustlers and people of the nightlife in Atlantic City. Each year, a king and queen were chosen from those who were living large and were popular in the night life. One evening, I just got back from New York around ten thirty with just enough cocaine and heroin to supply Buckey and Do Drop for two days. I kept a personal stash for myself until I could get back to New York. Mordy and Big Time, two friends of mine from D.C., were in town for two hours. They came straight to my apartment to wait for me. Stacey called them and other friends from New York, Philly, and beyond, to be in town that night. She invited them to witness me receiving the "king of the nightlife" crown because she had an inside track and knew I was going to be the winner.

That night, she gave me a cluster diamond ring in recognition of my success. We all sat at my usual ringside table at the Club Harlem while they called out the nominees for king of the nightlife. I heard them call my name as they called me to the stage to give me a trophy and put the crown on my head. The audience gave me tremendous applause with Morda and Big Time hollering the loudest. A lady named

Queenie was crowned the queen of the nightlife, and she got thunderous applause from the crowd because everyone knew and loved her. Queenie was known and loved by every pimp, hustler, con man, and celebrity who came through Atlantic City. Her reputation was so big that she landed a part in the movie *Atlantic City* starring Burt Lancaster after that night.

Very soon, I was like the proverbial sparrow that fell from the sky. I became addicted to my own product, spending my days and nights like a paranoid recluse. I was locked up in my own apartment, flipped out and tripped out on a mixture of heroin and cocaine. I had two pistols, all the doors and windows were locked, and I was waiting on somebody to come busting in on me at any minute. Since no one came, I ended up being my own best customer. Before long, I lost my car, and so-called friends began to distance themselves from me. I thought about how far I had fallen from living large in the hustler's world. My reign as king of the nightlife was as fleeting as a dream. The drugs that I hustled turned the tables on me. They sent me places I had never gone to commit crimes I had never done before. I took chances I never would have taken in the past. By this time, hardly any of the hustlers that were on their feet would have much to do with me. I was taboo, with the exception of a few that would come in from out of town and felt sorry for me. Occasionally, they would give me a little work, playing the confidence game or some other hustle to put some money in my pocket to help me get back on my feet. It never worked because I would blow money almost as fast as I got it. I preferred to burn it up rather than lie down and go to sleep with it.

One day, Pretty Melvin from Texas came in town for a few days. I had just bought an old work car for hustling after having taken a large sum of money on the gambling table one night. One of the men in the game had gotten broke and wanted to sell his car to have enough money to get back in the game. I bought it for seven hundred dollars. It was an old Chevy and wasn't much to look at but it would be a good car for hustling. He took his tags off so I needed to get my own tags. That night, I bought two tags from a dope friend name Butch to hold me over until I could get some legal ones. Two days later, Pretty Melvin and I had taken some money up near Delaware. We headed back toward Atlantic City, driving through a little town called Buena Vista. As I drove through this town, I knew from the past that I would be approaching a blinking caution light soon. As Pretty Melvin and I talked, I told him I was getting tired of the game. I was beginning to feel sorry for the people when I took their money.

He said, "If you really feel that bad about it, why don't you take your half and give it back to them?" I was quiet. After some time, he said, "Yeah, that's what I thought."

As I turned to look at him, I realized that I had just run that caution light without looking. At that moment, a car hit us, knocking us into a telephone pole that fell on top of the car and into a corner house living room. With the telephone pole on top of the car, Pretty Melvin and I were trapped inside. I could see the driver of the other vehicle that hit us. He was out of his car directing traffic. He came over to our car and asked if we were we all right. He told us to stay still because someone was calling an ambulance. The dashboard of the car was partly in my lap. I checked myself to see if I was cut or anything and then asked Melvin if he was okay. He said he was fine. I said to Melvin, "We need to get out of here before the police come."

We weren't that far from the people we had taken the money from earlier. Two or three young brothers pulled up and got out of a car to check us out. By this time, a large crowd had gathered around the car with people looking in telling us, "Hang on in there. Help is on the way!" Little did they know that Melvin and I didn't really want any help.

We asked the young boys to take us away from the accident. They said, "No, we can't do that! It's best you wait for an ambulance."

Somehow Melvin and I managed to get out of the car and slip through the crowd undetected. I don't know how we did it! We found an old man who was on an errand for his wife at the store up the street. We made him an offer he couldn't refuse to carry us on into Atlantic City from there. He thought we were stranded and knew nothing about the accident. We left the car. The tags were not mine anyway. We had a very close call that night.

I began having nightmares. Several nights a week, I would have the same dream of very long charter buses pulling alongside me. Suddenly, the doors would open and people with sticks, bats, chains, knives, and guns would jump out and chase me down the street. They would be shouting, "Get him! Get him! Get him!" I would wake up in a cold sweat. Sometimes the nightmares would be about giant bats trying to suck the blood from my neck while I fought them, touching and feeling their hair, claws, and teeth. I would wake up hollering and screaming.

After the car wreck, Pretty Melvin and I paid a guy to carry us out of town every day so we could work. One day, Melvin and I scored pretty good. He decided it was time for him to go back over to New York. He suggested it was time for me to go too. I agreed but I had another plan in mind. I decided I would buy another piece of car to get around in; this time, with tags and all. My plan was to go to New York only for one more dope package to put on the street. I would give it one last crack. I thought that I would get a good package of dope, turn it over three or four times, and leave town. I thought that I had it all figured out.

The next day, I bought a car, tags, insurance, and headed straight to New York to pick up several quarters of heroin. I bought some quinine, *benita*, and milk sugar for cutting the heroin. I got strainers, plastic measuring spoons, bags, and other paraphernalia then went to a hotel room on the Black Horse Pike in Atlantic City. I bagged up forty to fifty twenties to sell and gave out some samples just to let folk know that I was back in business. I had one last bit of business to attend to, and that was to pick up Little Gary. He would help me bag and move the rest of my dope. When I picked up Little Gary, I was on my way—or so I thought. Fate had other plans. As we headed up town on Baltic and Tennessee Avenue in Atlantic City, a city trash truck bolted out and hit my car. *Here we go once again!* I thought. *God must be trying to tell me something.*

We were shaken, dazed, and incoherent. People gathered around the car. It seemed like déjà vu all over again. "Y'all all right? Don't try to move. Somebody is calling the ambulance" came from the crowd that had gathered around the car.

I turned to see if Gary was okay and asked, "Man, you all right?"

He said, "Yeah, I'm all right. Just a little shaken up, that's all."

I told him we had to get out of there with all the dope we had in the car. The next thing I knew, the police had arrived asking if we were all right. "Yes, sir, just a little shaken up," we answered. Even though we had a good case for a lawsuit, we were in no position to take advantage of it with dope in the car.

The officer asked if we wanted to be taken to hospital. We told him no and that we would be alright. "Well, I think you'd better go. That was a pretty good hit you guys took. You never know about these things."

I said, "Yes, sir, but since my car is drivable, I'd rather drive myself to the hospital."

I didn't want to take any chances getting caught with the large quantity of heroin I was carrying. After the accident report was done, my first priority was to get rid of the dope and then drive to the hospital to be checked out. I was still a bit dazed from the hit we had taken. It seemed that we would have a pretty good case against the city for its truck running the light. We had several witnesses who would testify that it was not our fault. I picked up a female friend named Jean to hold the dope while we got checked out at the hospital.

Just as I had pulled up to the emergency entrance, I was pulled over by a police car. *Now what is this?* I thought. I showed my license and registration and explained to the officer that we had just been in an accident and we were at the hospital to be checked out.

"Everybody step out of the car," the officer said.

I held the small, brown candy bag that had my dope. I slowly got out of the car as the police canine unit pulled up. I positioned myself to be on the end as the three of us stood. We were directed to turn, put our hands on the car, and spread our legs so that we could be searched. As one officer began to search little Gary who was on the opposite end from me, I knew if I didn't make a break for it now with this dope, I would be going back to prison for a very long time. Even if they caught me with the dogs, I could get out of their sight long enough to get rid of it without them seeing me. *What did I have to lose?* I figured if I could make it to Atlantic Avenue a block away and turn the corner I might be able to get this dope off of me. I made a quick break for it, running as fast as I could as my friends were being searched.

One officer alerted the other, "We've got a runner!" One of the officers released a dog after me, running behind his dogs running after me.

As I turned the corner of Atlantic Avenue, I ducked between cars and looked for an opening in the traffic to cross the street. I turned to see the dog sliding on its paws as he turned the corner after me. Once I crossed the street, I turned another corner with the dog not far behind me. I saw a gutter a few yards from me so I faked a fall and tossed the dope into the gutter. I rolled away as far as I could as the dog turned the corner. As I was lifting myself from the ground, the dog leaped on me. We both fell to the ground, and the dog viciously bit me over and over. I wrestled him away from the gutter where I had tossed my dope.

The neighborhood people shouted at the officer who had now come around the corner, "Get that dog off him! Get that dog off him!"

The officer finally called the dog off of me. My shirt was ripped, my pants were torn, and my hands and legs were bleeding from the dog's bites. "Why did you run?" the officer asked.

"I don't know, officer. I guess I was a little scared and still in shock from the accident I just had."

"Well, let's try to get you to the hospital. You need a tetanus shot for these dog bites."

"Sir, while we are there, can you have them take some X-rays or something? I was going to the hospital in the first place for the accident I just had" I asked.

By this time, the dog bites didn't really matter. I was just relieved that they didn't catch me with that dope. The crowd around us was complaining about how they let the dog bite me and said they had better get me to the hospital. I thought the officer didn't have the slightest idea that I was running away from them because I didn't want to be caught with the dope I had on me. That would have brought me a twenty-year prison sentence easily. I was cuffed and taken straight to the hospital for the dog bites and shot. I thought I had outsmarted the police by getting rid of my drugs and that at worst they could only charge me for was resisting arrest.

When we arrived at the police station, I found out that we would all be charged for possession of cocaine. "What do you mean? I didn't have anything on me! How do you figure that?" I asked.

One of the officers stepped forward and said that while they had searched my car, they found a medicine bottle containing several capsules of cocaine hidden down in the back seat of my car where Jean had been sitting. She wasn't claiming it and neither was Little Gary so we were all charged with it. When we were all released on bail, I tried to appeal to Jean about taking the weight for what obviously belonged to her. I understood that she didn't want to go to prison but she would probably get probation if she would cop to it since she didn't have a record. What's more, it was hers anyway! It wasn't like she was taking the weight for what belonged to me. She would be taking the weight for what belonged to her. She would eventually take the weight, and got probation with a suspended sentence.

As for the car accident and possible suit against the city, I was just too busy trying to make ends meet. After we had gotten our cases resolved, I decided it would be a good time to get out of town. I needed to get away from the drugs that were taking a toll on me and the lifestyle that I couldn't seem to shake. I believed if I could get enough money to get a car and some fake jewelry to sell, I could make it with determination. My first decent piece of money came days after I made this decision. Before I could blow it, I thought that I would visit my brother Derek at the garage he owned where he fixed cars on the side in addition to working a full-time job at the Atlantic City Medical Center as a boiler engineer. Whenever I would go to visit Derek at his garage, he always seemed to have some type of car he was fixing up to sell. "Derek? Derek, where you at? You here?" I called out as I walked through the garage.

"Over here" he shouted from beneath the hood of a car in the middle of the garage. "Hey, bro, what's up? What you up to?"

"Man, I came by to see if you got a car I could buy. I need to get back out on the road. I believe if I could put some highway between me and Atlantic City, I could get back on my feet," I said.

"I got something I could let you have for about six hundred. That is about what I put into it getting it fixed," he said. He walked me over to the corner of the garage where he had an old car covered with a tarp. He pulled the tarp off. "Man, this is a good car. It may not look like much but this baby runs like a woman's stocking. I just rebuilt the motor in it." He turned the ignition key and said, "Listen at that motor, man." I didn't know what to listen for. When it came to cars and fixing stuff, I trusted my brother because he always took great pride in his work. "All I need to do is put two new tires on it and you'll be good to go."

Looking at the exterior of the car, you wouldn't think it could get you to the next block. The paint was chipped, and the hood was burnt orange. I saw rust spots all over the car, and you could see where most of the body of the car had been gold. The door on the driver's side had been blue but someone had attempted to paint over it with gold paint in an attempt to match it with the rest of the car. The entire body was just old.

"Man, if you want to wait a few days, I know a Hispanic guy who will paint the whole car for you for about three hundred," he offered.

"No, man. I don't want to stay around here that long. I'd like to be on the road sometime tomorrow. You think it could take me to the south?" I asked.

He said, "Man, I told you this is a good car. All you need is two new tires on the front and you can go anywhere."

23

TRYING AGAIN IN THE SOUTH

Although the car wasn't much to look at with two new tires, I was on the road headed south the next day. I figured by the time I got to the south, it would break down on me, but by then, I would have hustled enough money for another car. Somehow I believed that my salvation was in the south. Somehow I had this strange idea that the south would be my promised land. This would be the place where I could start all over again. The south would be the place where I would have another chance to do it right. I could prove to myself and the rest of the world that I was more than just an addict. I would hustle drug free. I would still sell fake jewelry, play craps and cards, and hustle pool. I wanted to be like normal folk and live happily ever after.

It never crossed my mind that starting over for normal people might mean getting a job ad finding new friends, new hang outs, a better philosophy to live by, and a change of direction. My thinking was not normal. As I made my way south, I hustled for days or sometimes weeks in places like Baltimore, Washington D.C., Richmond, Petersburg, Charlotte, and finally settled in Hickory, North Carolina.

The quality and quantity of drugs that I had been accustomed to was not available but white liquor was plentiful. I would indulge in it most weekends while playing three-card monte in a honky-tonk owned by a number man named Snow Ball. Rumor had it that Snow Ball shot and killed his wife. He served his time in prison and was now raising his two sons out of the honky-tonk. They were wild and carried pistols like their daddy. They were always ready to bring order whenever things got out of hand. That happened often on Friday and Saturday nights when the place was crowded. They had a kitchen counter where they served hot sandwiches, pickled pig's feet, and shot glasses of white liquor. Snow Ball would let me play three-card monte once the place got crowded and always look to get a percentage of my winnings. I didn't mind, especially since most people that come through carried a pistol. They would sometimes let it be known by shooting up into the ceiling.

On Friday and Saturday nights, I would be in Snow Ball's with a crowd gathered around the table, trying to find my red card as I gulped down a shot glass of white liquor to keep my nerves intact. Occasionally, someone would lose a bet by picking up the wrong card and would attempt to snatch their money back but I was always quicker, except for one time. A man snatched my money back and said he wasn't paying me. I punched him in the mouth and snatched my money out of his hand. He reached in his belt to pull a pearl-handled pistol, but before he could come out of his belt with it, Snow Ball shot up in the air and pointed his pistol at the man. He said, "I'm not gonna have this in my place. If you can't stand to lose, don't play in his game." The would-be shooter now eased his pistol back in his belt and walked away mouthing something.

Many other times, Snow Ball would come to my rescue when there were pistols involved. I never understood Snow

Ball. He carried a pistol, cussed like a sailor, drank white liquor, ran numbers, and gambled but was a faithful member of Mount Pisgah AME Church. He was in church every Sunday morning, dressed in a suit and carried a pistol. Snow Ball would usually close his place about midnight, and the crowd would move on down the street to the Talk of the Town or across town to Rat Bone's house, which was an after-hours joint. One Saturday afternoon while sitting in the barber's chair getting my haircut, I heard the barbers talking about the world's fair that was being held in Knoxville, Tennessee, that year. They were planning to take their families. I thought it might be a good idea to go with a load of watches and rings to take advantage of the large crowds. I ordered my shipment to be sent to Knoxville COD to pick up when I arrived. However, when I got to Knoxville, I found out that this was the last day of the fair and most people were headed back home. I decided I would stay in Knoxville for a few days until I sold most of my jewelry to make the time worthwhile. A few days later on the way back to Hickory, I stopped in a North Carolina town called Morganton to unload some of my jewelry, but I was arrested by a detective for larceny by trickery. It would be a few days before a friend would come from Hickory to get me out on bond.

Once I was out, I hustled and saved enough money to get the best attorney that money could buy because I didn't want to take any chances getting railroaded as I was from out of state. My attorney worked it out that I would take a guilty plea, get probation, pay court cost, and get a five-year suspended sentence. I really didn't look at this as a punishment or a hindrance. I took it as something that would help settle me down and stabilize me because that was something I really needed at that time. It would force me to become disciplined in my movements. The biggest problem I had was figuring out what I would do in a town like Hickory while being on probation. I needed something legal to keep me busy while I hustled my watches and played cards on the weekends.

I found an empty storefront that had two big cooking ovens with a counter, a few small tables, and some chairs. Once I talked to the owner and agreed on the rent, I was off and running. I got a certificate of occupancy and turned on the lights and water. I added a jukebox, a coin-operated pool table, and a coin-operated bowling machine. I went to talk with Snow Ball to get his blessing. He gave me his blessings and his white lightning connections too! To celebrate, he poured us each a bit of white liquor in a glass as he had done in times past. He told me how much he wished his sons were like me and that I reminded him of himself when he was a much younger man. He told me how much he regretted killing his two sons' mama. An occasional tear would drop into his glass of liquor as he would pull a handkerchief out to touch his eyes as if he were trying to keep the next tear from falling. I turned to put a quarter in the jukebox, pretending I hadn't noticed.

He taught me how to make sure I would have enough liquor to carry me through the night, what time I needed to be at the liquor store before closing, and what I needed to get. He also told me where to get my cases of beer at a good price. He really didn't mind the competition since he would usually close his place between eleven thirty and midnight. I was only open on Thursday, Friday, and Saturday night, and we stayed open until daybreak the next morning. I closed my pool table down about one in the morning to turn it into a crap table, paying someone to cut a percentage of the games for the house. Although I made a good piece of money after paying my helper, it still wasn't enough.

I didn't know it then, but it would take me many years to learn that my drug of choice was more and more of whatever made me feel good. More money, more drugs, and more of whatever would light my fire. I would leave town to hustle craps, cards, watches, and rings to make more money. I left others to run my little night spot until I returned to collect my money and would buy stock on Tuesday or Wednesday.

24

BACK TO PRISON IN NORTH CAROLINA

One night while coming through Charlotte, I was pulled over by the police doing a license check. They told me they had a warrant out for my arrest in Hickory. A million thoughts ran through my mind. *How could this be? As far as I knew I was clean, except for being on probation.* "What am I charged with, officer?"

"They say something about you being wanted for a larceny by tricking," he said.

"Oh no, that's the charge I'm on probation for, sir. I have already admitted to that," I pleaded.

"Well, we have to take you down to the station and arrest you anyhow. We have to hold you at least for seventy-two hrs. If Hickory doesn't come get you after that, we'll cut you loose."

After spending two days in the Mecklenburg county jail, two detectives came to take me back to Hickory on charges of larceny by trick. As they were driving me back to Hickory, I asked, "What am I charged with? I am already on probation for this charge in Morganton."

"We're not picking you up for that one. We're picking you up for another charge of larceny by trick. You seem to be the only one in the area who plays these kinds of games. This is your MO, and we aim to clear the books up on you for any other crimes committed like this. There's a guy in Hickory who says that you tricked him out of his money. You had told him you were selling TVs out of a house. He gave you his money for a TV. You went into the house and was supposed to bring a TV out, but you went out the back door of the house instead. He found out that you didn't live in the house, and nobody in the house knew you."

I laughed out loud. "I'm sorry, officer. That was *not* me," I said.

"Well, the guy you tricked believed that it was you," he said.

I thought, *How could this be?* I became quiet as we headed to Hickory. My mind went back to New York many years ago when I ran around with an old junkie name Willie who had taught me how to make money with old TVs that people throw away. We would clean them up, take the guts out, and put cinder blocks in the shell. Then we would carefully put on Zenith stickers, color stickers, and wrap them neatly in a cellophane wrap in nice taped-up Zenith, Magnavox, or Sony boxes. We would sell them off of a corner in Harlem. Our victims would have us lift them carefully into the trunks of their cars. It seemed like the stuff I had gotten away with in the past was now coming back to haunt me. This time, it really wasn't me, and I was willing to fight it in court to prove my innocence. After spending several months in the Catawba County Jail, I was ready for trial with my attorney feeling pretty good about my innocence. After the jury was seated, the victim took the stand, told his story of how he had been tricked out of his money, and never got the TV he paid for.

"Do you see the man in the courtroom that tricked you out of your money? Is he in here this morning?" the DA asked.

"Yes, he's here. Right over there!" He pointed a finger at me. That was easy since I was the only black man in the courtroom with an attorney. As the man stepped down, the witness for the state took his seat to tell what had happened. This was a tall black man who appeared to be at least six foot one or six two. I had never seen him before in my life and didn't know him from a can of paint. They produced a composite drawing, which he helped the police create of the man who had swindled his friend. This was exhibit number one.

The prosecutor paraded the picture before the jurors. It was a man with a large Afro and dark features. Then turning to the witness, he asked, "Is this the picture you helped the officers draw of the man who swindled your friend?"

The witness pointed at me and said, "Yes, but he's not the one. The man was much darker than him and as about as tall as I am. That's not the one."

I asked my attorney to motion for dismissal. "Dismissal denied. It's not this man who lost his money. It's the other one," said the judge. Turning to the witness, he asked, "Did anybody talk to you today about this case?"

"No, sir. That's not him," he answered.

"Take your seat," said the judge. "Call the next witness."

The next witness for the state was the officer who went to the scene of the crime after the call was made. According to the police report, the perpetrator was described as a very dark-skinned male that was six feet tall or taller.

My attorney asked the officer, "Is this the report you wrote?"

"Yes, it is," said the officer.

My attorney questioned the officer, "You have here in your report that the man who took the gentleman's money was a very dark-skinned male. Look at Mr. Longcrier. Does he look very dark-skinned to you?"

The officer answered, "Yes, he does."

My attorney asked, "If he looks very dark-skinned to you, how would you describe a black male who is darker than him?"

He answered, "I don't know, but he sure looks dark-skinned to me." I glanced over at the jurors to see if there was any hint of disbelief on their faces since I am far from being very dark-skinned.

My attorney continued pressing the officer. "I see further on your report, you wrote that the man was six feet tall or taller."

"That is correct," the officer replied.

My attorney then turned to me and said, "Mr. Longcrier, would you stand up please?" I stood, half smiling to myself because it was obvious I was no more than five feet and a half at best. I was as far from being six feet or taller as I was from being very dark-skinned. The attorney asked the officer, "Look at Mr. Longcrier. Does he look six feet tall to you?"

The officer looked me up and down, turned to my attorney, and said, "By God, he does to me."

I was in such shock and disbelief that I don't remember anything else that was said that day by my attorney or anyone else. The second shock came after the jury deliberated for two and a half hours, coming back with a guilty verdict. I was stunned.

My mind took me back many years to the New Jersey State Prison while serving time in Rahway. I met a man there named Thompson who spent six years on death row prior to the electric chair being abolished when his sentence was changed to life. He was accused of killing an elderly white woman while breaking into her home. The witness had given the police the description of a tall, white male or a tall, light-skinned black male. Thompson fit the latter description but he had just gotten off work the night of the murder and did not have time to be at the murder scene. He had coworkers and supervisor as witnesses, and he consistently proclaimed his innocence. He was picked up by the police as he walked home that night from work charged with this horrific crime, found guilty, and sentenced to die in the electric chair. I thought about how he must have felt. Never in my wildest dreams had I thought that this could ever happen to me.

As if someone threw a bucket of cold water on my head, I was suddenly back in the courtroom. The judge dismissed the jury and decided on a sentence of five years in the North Carolina Department of Corrections. I asked my attorney to appeal. The motion was granted and an appeal bond was set. I would try to work fast to make bond. *I won't lose in the court of appeals*, I thought to myself. I had some money on me so I asked Big Rosey to call around to find a bondsman to get me out, but nobody wanted to touch me. It sounded to them that the charge of larceny by trick was like working black magic or witchcraft. To make matters even worse, I was from out of state. Big Rosey was determined to get me out. She was the best friend I had in Hickory. When I called her on the phone from the jail, she assured me she would have me out by Christmas. That was just a few weeks away.

Big Rosey was the most faithful and loyal friend a person could have in their corner while the chips where down. She made her living as a professional and a notorious shoplifter. Her picture had been posted in just about every mall and most clothing stores around town. She would carry a notebook with a laundry list of orders that people had placed with her for merchandise such as suits, sweaters, slacks, dresses, and coats along with size and color. She collected money from her "customers" on Thursdays and Fridays. This was how she made a living despite being known by every store merchant, cop, and bail bondsman. One day, I asked Big Rosie how she got started stealing. She told me that when she was a little girl in about the third or fourth grade, the teachers would make fun of her because she had a speech impairment. She could hardly pronounce her own name, read, or write. Instead of trying to teach her, they would laugh at her. Sometimes they would go get other teachers to laugh with them. She told me that it hurt her so bad she wanted to do something to hurt them back so she decided to start stealing their pocketbooks to get even. I guess she had been trying to get even ever since because she never did learn to talk, read, or write very well, but she sure was good at stealing.

Since Big Rosie knew all of the bondsman, she was able to convince one to take a chance on me because she had done a lot of business in merchandise with him. He helped me with the condition that I pay double the amount of the cost for the bond. This would be six thousand cash since I was from out of state. This cash would be divided with another bondsman who would come in also to share the risk if I ran. It seemed fair enough to me, but my big problem was I only have about half of that amount. Big Rosie convinced me she would get the rest of the money somehow and have me out by Christmas as she had promised but I had to promise that I would pay her back.

A week before Christmas, two bondsman were at the jail to post my bond along with Big Rosie and her share of the bond money. They were two of the most notorious bondsman around. I saw them waiting on me to fill out their paperwork. One had a reputation for changing his mind once he had gotten you out and have you locked back up again. People said that he had a man's bond that didn't quite have all of his money with the understanding that his grandmother would pay the rest of the money once he brought him to the house. While the bondsman was en route to take the man to his grandmothers, he told the man that he had to make a stop on the way to get his potatoes picked before it got too cold and that if he would help him, he would get home sooner. The man ended up picking potatoes throughout the day and eating a bologna-and-cheese sandwich the bondsman fixed for him. The man didn't mind it much because he knew once he was finished, he was free anyhow. The bondsman didn't have to take a chance on him so he was grateful. To the man's surprise, once he was finished picking potatoes that day, the bondsman said that he had changed his mind about going his bond and that he was carrying him back to jail. Once the bondsman got him back to the jail, he informed the man that he owed $1.50 for the bologna and cheese sandwich that he had eaten for lunch at his house.

Once I had signed all of the bond papers they had for me, they began to read me the riot act. They began to tell me what they would do to me if I ran. They threatened to hunt me down and find me no matter what it took. They would be working hard for their money because I had every intention of running if I didn't win my case in the appeals court. My attorney thought that I had a pretty good chance based on the flimsy evidence they had against me. In the meantime, I made sure to keep my promise and pay Big Rosie the money she had put up for me. Eventually, I ended up losing my appeal and becoming a fugitive from justice. I reasoned that I was a fugitive from injustice because this was a crime I had not committed. My attitude was to let them catch me if they can because I was in no way ready to go to prison to serve a five-year sentence for a crime I had not committed. The following year, I was picked up in Atlantic City and extradited back to North Carolina to start serving time on the five-year sentence. I was first brought to a prison in Salisbury, North

Carolina, which was called High Rise. It had about eleven or twelve floors with nine hundred to twelve hundred inmates. This was where most of the new entry inmates would come from throughout the state for orientation, shots, a number of tests, and a state number. This was not new to me since this was how most of the institutions that I had been in operated.

I always dreaded them taking my blood since all of the veins in both my arms and legs had literally collapsed because of my intravenous abuse of heroin and cocaine. Now some doctor or nurse would have to tinker around sticking me with needles as if I was a pin cushion trying to find a vein. After a couple of months in the High Rise, I was sent to another prison called Craggy up in western North Carolina. The French Broad River ran in front of it with a large mountain in the back. It had steps built into the mountain that the inmates would climb when going to the yard to play basketball, lift weights, or other activities during yard time. Older convicts called this prison The Rock. It was eventually torn down. My job assignment was with one of the many road gangs they had to keep us busy. We would cut out roads, paths, and underbrush with chainsaws and bush axes. We would cut down trees like lumber jacks with two guards nearby holding shotguns on each end. We had a gang boss named Mad Thad who carried a pistol in his hip pocket and had a mouthful of tobacco. My deepest concern was one of the guards with the shotgun named Smitty who was said to be a Vietnam vet. He seemed to be a little shell-shocked. He wore dark sunglasses and what appeared to be a little boy's hat with ear muffs. He had an itchy trigger finger and would shoot anything or anybody that made a move or a noise that didn't seem right to him. I would always work where I could keep a good eye on Smitty because you couldn't tell which way he was looking because of the dark glasses he wore. I didn't want him to make the mistake of shooting me for no reason.

It wasn't unusual to find yourself hanging off the side of some mountain with a rope tied around your waist and a bush axe in your hand cutting underbrush. Some days we would be cutting out paths while battling snakes, poison ivy, or poison oak. I kept wondering how I got there and what scheme could I create to get out of this. They should have given me a job in the kitchen, laundry, or some other type of job besides the road gang. They should have at least given me some type of orientation about how to identify poison ivy or poison oak and what to do should you get bitten by a snake. Some of the guys were from the mountains and knew all that stuff. Instead of running from snakes, some of these guys would run to the snake! They would tell me how they made a living catching snakes and selling their skins. I was a city boy so there was nothing in my background that prepared me for what was happening now.

One morning, I decided that I had *had* enough of this stuff. I decided that I would tell the sergeant who was calling the gangs out that morning that I was too sick to go out and I needed to see the doctor. Later I found out that this sergeant was the most notorious officer in the prison. He was a baby-faced sergeant named Angel who had been hardened after spending many years as a prison guard before being promoted to sergeant. After I told him I was sick that morning, he told me to stay in so that I could see the doctor. Before I knew it, they were calling me to get my stuff. Sergeant Angel gave them orders to lock me up in the hole because he took a good look at me and I didn't appear sick to him. He thought that he would have me locked up for a few days for not wanting to work. Two days later, I was let out of the hole. The following morning, I was called to report to work.

After Sergeant Angel called my gang out that morning, he pulled me to the side and said, "Longcrier, I want you to know that if you ever get sick again, I'm gonna put you back in that hole, you hear?"

"Yes, sir," I said.

In spite of my efforts to apply for other jobs in the prison, Sergeant Angel made sure that I was kept on the road gang for the rest of the time I was there. When I first arrived at Craggy, I was assigned a locker and a top-bunk bed. One day, I wandered into the dayroom where a few inmates sat watching the news on TV. As I was taking in my surroundings, another inmate came in shortly after me. He took one look at what was on the TV. He decided that he wasn't interested in watching that so he switched the channel to something he wanted to watch. I was prepared for a fight to break out because this was something you don't do in prison—at least, not where I was from. However, the men that were watching the news never said a word. They just got up from their seats and walked out. I knew then I would have to do this time, staying away from the TV if I wanted to stay out of trouble.

I decided that I would start reading my Bible more and some other books that had been passed on to me from a Seventh Day Adventist inmate that I had met while in the Salisbury prison. I marveled at the wisdom of Solomon in the book of Ecclesiastes and Proverbs. I studied the teachings of the Adventists with five or six other inmates in the evenings and attended Chaplain Frank Shirley's worship services three or four nights a week. I started taking several Bible correspondences courses, and I thought I was getting closer to God. On Sundays during visiting hours while they called the names of inmates who had visits, I would go to sleep because I knew no one was coming to visit me.

One day, one of the Adventist inmates saw that I didn't get any visits and told me about a man named Mr. Jim who was one of the Adventist Christian volunteers. He would come and visit different inmates each week. They told me that he would visit me too if I wrote to him. I wrote Mr. Jim, telling him who I was, where I was from, and how I had ended up in the situation I was in being such a long way from home. I really didn't have anybody to come visit. Other inmates told me that he visited inmates who had no visitors. I asked him to consider pulling me out on a visit if he could. The next week, I got a letter from Mr. Jim asking me to put him on my visitor's list. Before Mr. Jim could visit me at the Craggy prison, the programmers told me to get ready to ship out to the Watauga Correctional Center, which was a prison in Boone, North Carolina.

25

MY TRANSFORMATION
BEGINS

This was not the transfer that I had hoped for because I had requested to be transferred to Catawba County! When I heard they were sending me to Boone, I asked some of the other inmates on the block to tell me about it. "Man, that's further up in the mountains! That's a lock-up honor grade where they send most nutcases," they said.

I thought, *How could they have made such a grave mistake? Why are they sending me to a place like this? Had I done something or did they see something in my psychiatric evaluation to make them think that I needed to go there?* Maybe Sergeant Angel did this to me because I played sick to get out of work. One of the Christian inmates I studied with suggested I go and talk to the prison chaplain to see if he could stop the transfer. I already pleaded and complained to the program staff all the way to the warden of the prison.

Chaplain Shirley was my last hope. I explained to the chaplain what had happened, but he just gently patted my shoulder and said, "Now, son, don't do anything to get yourself in trouble. They've probably made a mistake in sending you to Boone, but it's too late to do anything about it now.

Once you get there, put in a request to see the warden. I know him. He's a good Christian man. He'll realize that they made a mistake in sending you there. You probably won't be there more than a couple of weeks. They will send you where you were supposed to go."

Chaplain Shirley was very mild-mannered. He convinced me everything would work out just like he said it would. The following day, I was on the transfer bus with inmates who were being dropped off at other prisons. When they got to my stop, I was the only inmate called to get off at this prison. I thought that was unusual because at most stops, several inmates got off at the same time. I got my bag with all my belongings and looked up to see a big, bulky officer coming down the walkway to receive me. Behind the officer was a tall, high-stepping white inmate wearing black state-issued glasses with thick Coke-bottle lenses. The officer frisk searched me and told the inmate to take me to the sergeant's office where I would check in.

The inmate extended a long arm to shake my hand, saying, "Welcome to the Starship Enterprise. We go to galaxies where no man has gone before."

I immediately realized what the inmates told me about this place back at Craggy. This was the minimum-security prison where they placed most of the nutcases. What was I going to do? Before the week was out, I decided to follow a handful of inmates to a Bible study class that was being held in the prison chapel. I figured the best thing I could do was pass my time studying the Scriptures. One of the volunteers asked an inmate from my block to open the class with prayer. This inmate prayed with the elegance and passion of a preacher. His participation in the class and knowledge of the Scriptures was impressive. I decided to talk to him once we got back to the block. Perhaps I could learn a lot from this guy. I thought he and I were probably the two sanest inmates in our block. Once back in the block, I introduced myself to him and told him I was impressed with his knowledge of the Scriptures. I asked him to advise me about the best scriptures to read to get closer to the Lord. What followed caught me completely off guard.

He told me he had been there for eight years and that he had been an insurance salesman before his incarceration. One night, he was on his way home after making his rounds. He sensed something was over his head and looked up to see a flying saucer. He said he began running as the flying saucer followed from above. It caught up with him and hit him on the top of his head, knocking him unconscious. When he woke up, he saw the saucer just above his head and watched the doors open. He heard little green men saying to one another, "Let's take him to the planet." He said he got up and ran as fast as he could until he wound up at the front door of someone's home. He was hollering and shouting for them to let him in because he had been hit in the head by a flying saucer.

I realized that I was talking to crazy man. How could I exit the conversation as if we were talking normally? I excused myself to write a letter that I had to get out before the second shift officer went off duty. I offered to resume the conversation another time. I kept pretty much to myself after that and focused on my job at a landfill working in a plant that recycled old cans. After thirteen months in Boone, I was finally sent to Catawba Correctional Center in Newton North Carolina. My elderly aunt Bea visited me. Occasionally, Mr. Jim came with Adventist literature for me to read. I continued studying scripture and doctrine of the Adventists and taking every Bible correspondence course I could get my hands on. I remember studying those courses like a crossword puzzle. I even debated Adventist doctrine in the prison with many of the more advanced Christians, not realizing that I knew very little about God. I found out that despite my knowledge of the Scriptures, I could still fail miserably in the self-control department. I used to bring sardines from the prison commissary back to my block. They would leave a lingering odor if you just threw the can unwrapped into the trash can in the block. The dorm man had a problem if you left these sardine cans around for him to clean up. I would always wrap my sardine cans in a newspaper and then put them in the trash outside of the dorm so he would not have to deal with it. I knew how he felt about these cans being left around for him to clean up.

Several other inmates liked to eat sardines as much as I did, but they couldn't care less about the dorm man or anybody else having to come behind them and clean them up. One day, another guy finished eating a can of sardines but left them on the dorm table, smell and all. The dorm man had a fit! He came down to my bunk raising cane and pointing a finger in my face. He threatened what he would do to me the next time I left one of those sardine cans lying around for him to clean up after me. He knew that I never left my cans around for him to pick up. I always made it a point to wrap mine up in newspaper and toss them in the can outside the dorm. He knew who left their cans around. They were practically daring him to say anything to them. It wasn't fair that he decided to make me the scapegoat of his wrath. He and everybody else in the dorm knew that I was trying to be a good Christian. I was on my bunk reading my Bible and minding my own business. I think he figured since I was trying so hard to be a good Christian, I would be the one most likely to let it go.

However, the doctrine that I debated on the prison yard could not restrain me from grabbing his neck and pinning him to the bars. Other inmates ran over to pull me away. "It ain't worth it, man. Let it go!"

I gradually released my grip. "I told you, man, those cans weren't mine so you better watch yourself!"

He opened his mouth to speak with a frightened look on his face and said, "Man, I thought you were supposed to be a Christian. You can't be no Christian acting like that. You ain't no different from the rest of these guys, and you're walking around here carrying a Bible."

I thought, *Maybe I'm not a Christian after all. What happened to me?* After all of that studying, all those correspondence courses I had taken, all the scriptures I had memorized, and all of the Bible studies and church services I had attended, I totally lost my self-control. It was the first test, the first chance, and the first opportunity to prove that I was a Christian, and I blew it. I had failed miserably. Did I really know God or did I just know a little of the Bible? Despite this setback, I continued to press toward the mark of God for a higher calling. I was faithful in my studies. I consistently attended Sunday school and worship in the little trailer where we held our services at Catawba Correctional Center.

I met some of the best prison ministry volunteers this side of heaven—Mr. Jim Goforth, Mr. Ron Spencer, and Mr. Frances Orders. These guys would make a spiritual imprint on me that would last a lifetime. Although they were from different churches, their dedication to come faithfully to the prison every Sunday was impressive. They brought the gospel of Matthew 25:36 into the prison every Sunday morning, "When I was in prison, you came unto me." They also modeled Christ by the way they taught us. This is the Christ that I later began to see and look for in the Bible and in the behavior of people who claimed to be Christians. It is no wonder that they called the early Christians "people of the way."

In order to leave an impression on a bunch of hard-core convicts, your ways carry more weight than your words. I tried my best to live in keeping with the teaching of the Scriptures, but while my spirit was willing, my flesh was weak. The consistency of prison ministry volunteers is extremely important because you never know when a person is ready to change. I had been in prison so many times but wasn't ready to change. Like so many others, I wasn't ready to hear the gospel message carried by prison ministry volunteers but they kept coming anyway. I thank God for their dedication and faithfulness. It takes a special kind of person to be a prison ministry volunteer because they plant seeds that may take years to produce the fruit of change in a heart like mine. When I was ready, they were there. They stuck by me to help me through the struggle of change.

I found out that it was easier to live as a Christian in prison than outside in society. When I was released, I came to grips with character defects that were dormant while I was incarcerated. I got a job but each day became harder and harder. I had to get used to being free, going to work, having money in my pockets, bored to death, counting the hours before quitting time, and then getting up the next morning to start the same routine all over again. I remember thinking I was not making much progress. At the pace I was getting paid, it would be a long time before I could get another car, some clothes, and my own place instead of staying with my elderly aunt Bea in Hickory, North Carolina. I still wanted to be a Christian, live normally, and stay out of trouble. So I came up with the bright idea that I would quit my job, lay my religion down for a while, and do what I knew to do to get some faster money. I would get a car, get my wardrobe together, and have enough money to keep me going for a while. When I was back on my feet, I would get another job, pick up my religion, start going to church on Sunday, and live happily ever after.

It wasn't long before I was back into my old lifestyle, which gradually led me back to my drug addiction. As my addiction escalated, I lost a tremendous amount of weight. I was living from pillar to post, spending the night in one city after another on somebody's couch or maybe finding a spot on the floor of a dog's house to camp out for the night. I hadn't had enough yet I was powerless to stop myself. I was like a runaway train. Who could stop me? I hadn't planned on it turning out like this. I searched my mind for a scripture but couldn't find any. Nothing I had studied and debated on the prison yard helped me in my misery. Even though I really meant it when I gave my life to the Lord, all the evidence of my Christianity seemed to have vanished—except for one thing, I really didn't want to live this way anymore. I really wanted to live right. If I could just get another chance to start clean and try it again, I would make it this time. I thought I just needed a little rest. Something in me believed if I could be locked up somewhere for a little time, I could get it. I didn't need a long time, just a short sentence.

Although I couldn't remember any scripture to help me, I decided to pray. It was a rather odd prayer for an addict but it was sincere. It was the only prayer I could pray for myself at that time. I prayed, "Lord, I need some more time in jail or prison. Not a long time. Just enough time to get the drugs out of my system, nurse my body back to health, rest, and get closer to you. If you will answer this prayer for me, I will make it this time." Each time I got broke or found myself in some situation that I had no business in, this would be my prayer. I prayed this prayer until God answered it but not in the way that I expected. I committed the crime of larceny through trickery by convincing a man to take money out of his bank in exchange for something I didn't have. Once I was arrested for this crime, they wanted to try me as a habitual felon. This meant I could receive a fourteen-year-to-life sentence because of the Habitual Felon Act. A fourteen-year-to-life sentence! I had been praying to God for some more time, but this much time wasn't really what I had in mind.

I couldn't afford an attorney because I was flat broke so they assigned a public defender to take my case. On our first visit, he told me that things didn't look good for me because the guy I had tricked was too ashamed to tell anybody the real truth. He was accusing me of robbing him at gunpoint. This was a lie because a gun was not involved. The attorney said he would do the best that he could and talk to the prosecutor. The next visit with my attorney was worse than the first. "Mr. Longcrier, the prosecutor wants to sentence you to fourteen years to life for the Habitual Felon Act."

My first reaction was to ask if a deal was on the table because in most cases, a felon would be offered to take a lesser charge and a reduced sentence. This would avoid a trial, which would save the courts time and money. However, in my case, no deal was offered. My attorney said that the judge was the worst one for my case and that he had intended to prosecute me to the fullest extent of the law. Fourteen years to life was far too much time to do for the crime that I had committed, even though I was more than a three-time loser as a convicted felon.

What do I do now? I thought. If I could make bond, I could run, but I had no money and nobody to post my bond. I was more than five hundred miles away from home. I literally burned all of my bridges behind me. My whole life went before me in a panoramic vision. The people I had hurt, the drugs I had used, and the jails and prisons where I served time all flashed before my eyes. I asked myself, "Is this how it ends? Is this how the game will pay me off? Am I doomed to be a bug in a matchbox? After all the years of hustling, trying to pave my way to fame, and taking the slick shortcuts, this is how I end up?"

When I was faced with a fourteen-year-to-life sentence, I just about asked God to take my life. I was hopeless. God heard my prayer and answered. "I'll take your life but not in the way you mean. Son, I'm going to make you do something you've never done before. I'm going to make you ask me to help you." I vaguely remember the attorney leaving that afternoon saying something to the affect that he would try to see what else he could do, but the sound of his voice did not encourage me. All I could do now was pray. I told God I was sorry for making such a mess of my life. I was sorry for the things that I had done to people and the pain I brought upon my family and friends. I asked God to forgive me. If God would come into my life and make something out of the mess I made, I promised to give him back a man after his own heart.

As I continued to pray for God to fix the broken, damaged parts of my life, I found myself not praying for release from a long prison sentence, but a closer relationship with him. I needed the peace of his presence. As time went on, I continued to pray in this fashion day and night. Sometimes another inmate in the block would pass my cell and catch me in prayer while lying on my bunk and staring straight up at the ceiling. I would quickly cut my prayer off for fear that they might think I was losing it. I also prayed for relief from the horrible nightmares that woke me up screaming some nights. I was so ashamed of my life that all I dared to ask God for was grace.

It was two weeks before I heard from my attorney again. I was just getting my lunch tray with a small chicken leg, some mashed potatoes, green beans, some tea, and a slice of cake. I heard, "Longcrier? Longcrier? Where is Longcrier?"

"Over here!" I called out. I was just getting ready to taste my mashed potatoes when I saw my attorney looking as if he had just hit the lottery.

He said, "Looks like today is your lucky day. We have a new judge on the bench this afternoon. I've been talking to him and the prosecutor about your case. They seem to be getting a big laugh out of it. This judge has been around and he has seen these crimes before. He knows no pistol was involved. He sent me with these papers for you to sign. If you plead guilty to misdemeanor larceny, he'll bring you in court this afternoon and give you a two-year sentence. Tomorrow, the other judge will be back on the bench. This judge was brought in this afternoon to take his place until tomorrow."

I wasted no time, saying, "I'll take it! Where do I sign?"

The attorney rushed out with the papers for my plea bargain in his hand and went back to the courtroom. I was so happy that I gave my mashed potatoes, green beans, and chicken to another inmate. Nobody but God could make it possible for things to turn out the way they did. God heard my prayers, read my heart, and gave me mercy. After sentencing, I was immediately shipped out to McClainville Correctional Center for forty five days and then shipped to another prison called Danbury. At this point, it didn't matter where they sent me since I was already several states away from home. I wasn't really looking for anybody to come and visit me this far away. I was too ashamed to even write a letter to let anybody know I was back in prison again.

However, this time, I got a new perspective on my life. I understood where Eldridge Cleaver was coming from in his classic memoir *Soul on Ice*. He said that after he returned to prison, he took a long look at himself. For the first time in his life, he admitted that he was wrong. He admitted that he had gone astray, not so much from the law as from being human or civilized. He began to write to save himself. My salvation and sanity came from constant reading of the scriptures. I attended every church service, every Bible study, and took every Bible correspondence course that I could get my hands on. I was so absorbed in my studies that I didn't think much about being released. Before I was only studying the Scriptures with my head, but now I was studying them with my head and my heart.

After spending a few months in Danbury, I was shipped to McCain Prison Hospital to work in the kitchen. The prison hospital had inmates who were paralyzed in wheelchairs, gunshot victims, and terminally ill needing surgery. I worked in the kitchen on the line as a server, cleaning, mopping, or doing other odd jobs. I really didn't like it but nothing mattered much while I continued to lose myself in my studies. I also exercised every day on the yard and played chess, one of my favorite forms of recreation. After I beat most of the guys who would sit in front of me on the chess board, everybody wanted me to play a guy named Corey because he was supposed to be the best in the prison. Corey couldn't come to the yard much except on certain days because he was in a wheelchair. He heard that I could play, and I was looking forward to playing him. He sent word to me to meet him on the yard on Saturday morning. When they called "Yard out!" that Saturday, I beat Corey in the first game. We finished playing before they called "Yard in!" This didn't go over too well with Corey since a lot of inmates were out on the yard that morning just to watch us play. Soon the word spread throughout the prison that I beat Corey at chess. It even got to Corey's supervisor who was over at the clothes house where Corey worked. Corey told him that he would beat me the next time we played.

The following Tuesday, Corey and I met on the yard. I beat him two in a row before they called yard in. Corey asked me where I worked, and I told him in the kitchen. He said, "How would you feel if I got you transferred out of the kitchen to the clothes house where I work? We need another man down there. Plus, I've got a chess set on the job."

It sounded too good to be true because the rule said you have to be in the kitchen at least six months before going to any other job, especially since everybody that came in with me from Danbury was brought there because they needed more men in the kitchen. Corey swiveled around in his wheelchair and said he would have me out of the kitchen before the week was out. The next day, a tall blonde man in civilian clothes walked into the chow hall asking the inmates to find me. One of the inmates pointed me out on the line serving. "Your name Longcrier?" he asked.

"Yes, sir," I answered. "Well, I'm Corey's supervisor. He tells me you got lucky and beat him on the chess board. He thinks that he can beat you so I'm transferring you to the clothes house so y'all can play when y'all are not busy. You'll start Monday morning, and I'll make the arrangements with the kitchen supervisor."

Sure enough, Monday morning, I started working in the clothes house. My job was to pick up the dirty linen on the tiers, pass out clean linen, and change out the prison uniforms and underwear once a week. I was also responsible for dressing inmates when they were going home or to court. Corey and I played chess almost every day during our down-time. I had the sweetest job in the joint because I was a pretty good chess player.

I continued studying Scripture, praying, and thanking God for his many blessings. One day, they called me to the programmer's office. "Today is your lucky day. We just got a call from Raleigh saying to terminate your sentence and let you go free."

I was so taken back. I almost asked them to let me stay one more day. It seemed like everything was happening so fast and all at once. I didn't have any money. I didn't have any clothes to wear and wasn't sure where I could go, especially since no one was expecting me. All I remember is that they furnished me with a bus ticket to Greensboro and $3.50 that I had earned working in the clothes house that week. Corey found a pair of shoes, some slacks, shirt, and underwear from the clothes house. I got in a prison van and went directly to the bus station to board a bus to Greensboro. I couldn't believe I was free! Just six months before, I was faced with a fourteen-year-to-life sentence and no way out.

From Greensboro, I caught a ride to Hickory to live with my elderly great-aunt Ms. Beatrice Roberts again. She was a member of Friendship Baptist Church for more than fifty years and played the organ in her church. The community loved her, and she was well-known for founding the 100-Voice choir with members from churches throughout the area. Aunt Bea was also blessed to have a piano in her home. Many times, visitors dropped in to rehearse a song or just to sing while she played the piano. Aunt Bea had been caring for her eldest sister Odessa who was approaching a hundred years old at that time. She and Aunt Bea had a wonderful sense of humor and were always teasing or telling a funny story that was sure to make you laugh. In the morning, Aunt Bea would always cook breakfast such as corn fritters, eggs, ham, bacon, lots of cinnamon rolls, cheese grits, and other tasty dishes. At night, we would enjoy ice cream, cake, watch a little TV, and then turn in for the night. Also, in the house was Boardwalk Bill, the one-time pool shark who first introduced me to the world of pool-hall hustlers. He retired back home in the south to draw a monthly check and sang in the senior choir at Morningstar First Baptist Church.

Now that I was out, my first order of business was to get some clothes. I presented this problem to Aunt Bea. She pointed me in the direction of Aunt Odessa who was not only a hundred years old, but had a 1929 concept of money. Odessa's husband Fritz left her in pretty good shape. It had been more than twenty years since he passed away, leaving her with eighty-seven acres of land and enough money for her to live off the interest. She was what they called well-to-do.

One evening while she was knitting quietly, I seized the opportunity to ask her for a loan for some clothes until I got a job. She reached into her pocketbook for a small purse with zippers. She took out a ten-dollar bill. She then grabbed my hand, gently placed it in my palm, and said, "I want you to get a couple dress shirts, a new tie, a suit for church, underwear, and socks. You be sure to bring me my change back, you hear?" At first, I thought she was kidding with me as she often did, but judging from the expression on her face, I could see that she was as serious as a heart attack. When I told her that this would hardly be enough money to buy these things, she simply said that this wasn't her money. This was her dead husband Fritz's money, and she couldn't be spending his money like that. If I hadn't known better, I would have thought that he was still alive. She closed the zipper to her purse and stuck it back into her pocketbook. I knew then that this was all the money I was going to get that day. Then she said, "What you think this is, boy? You must think money grows on trees around here." I burst out laughing until she began to laugh with me.

She told me to go to the Goodwill store in town and find something nice because she often found pretty good deals there. I learned a very valuable lesson in money management that day because I found almost everything I needed in the Goodwill store with the exception of the suit and the coat. I bought a really nice pair of shoes for $2.50, some shirts, some slacks, some underwear, a belt, and a tie with change left over. This was the first of many Goodwill runs to come. I rushed back to the house to tell Aunt Odessa about the great bargains I found at the Goodwill store. I was, in some strange way, feeling proud of myself because in times past I would have preferred to take the risk of stealing some new clothes or some illegal maneuver to get enough money to buy new clothes. Now here I was, learning to look for bargains at Goodwill with ten dollar. This is what the songwriter must have had in mind when she wrote, "Now I know I've been changed, and the angels in heaven done signed my name."

I went to church every Saturday because Mr. Jim would send someone to pick me up and take me to worship at the Seventh-day Adventist Church. He had been nice to me during my incarceration, encouraging me, and keeping me up with new study materials. He really wanted to see me get off to a good start once I was released. On Sundays, I'd go to church with Aunt Bea. She was proud to take me to her church and told everyone that she was my North Carolina mama. Every day, I would pound the pavement looking for work. Sometimes I made repeat trips to places where I had already been. I would hear things like, "Weren't you just here the other day? Didn't we tell you we had no openings? Didn't we tell you we weren't hiring?" I would say, "Yes, but I just thought maybe someone had got fired or quit since then."

Once I was sent from Manpower to a soft drink bottling plant. I was sitting at the desk when the call came in needing someone to load trucks with crates of sodas. The Manpower worker asked me if I could load crates. "Of course I can!" I said. I had just gotten out of prison and I was in the best shape of my life because I had been lifting weights on the yard and exercising every day. This was right up my alley. I could load soda crates on a truck if I couldn't do anything else. The worker told the soft drink company people that he was sending me right away. He handed me a slip to take with me that said, "Looks like you got the job. They're waiting on you."

When I arrived, the woman looked me up and down and said, "Can I help you?"

"Yes, ma'am. I was just sent from Manpower to apply for the job loading soda trucks. I'm the one that they spoke to you about over the phone." It was obvious from the look on her face that I was not what she had expected. She stumbled to gather her composure and asked if I had any experience in loading soda trucks. I thought, *How much experience do you need to load a soda truck except to be in shape to do some lifting?* I tried to assure her that I was in the best of shape, I was a quick learner, and a hard worker. I told her that I needed and wanted to work. She could count on me, and I would not let her down if she gave me the job. "Ma'am, I know you need somebody. I was sitting there when you called in. Why not give me a try?"

I was determined not to let her off the hook, but she was just as determined not to let me have the job. She said, "While you were on your way over, the guy who had the job before you came by and said that he was going to keep the job. He has a lot of experience loading trucks. I'm sorry we wasted your time."

In times past, this would be where I would get off the right track and start hustling again. I would be the one in control of the situation. I would be the one to determine whether I would go to work or not. Sometimes I would purposely blow a job opportunity so that they wouldn't hire me but this time, I really wanted to work. I began to feel like the boy who cried wolf when no wolf was coming. Finally, a real wolf appears and no one will come to the rescue. I was determined not to be discouraged and continued to look for work every day. Rain or shine, I was more determined than ever. I had no thought or desire to do anything else but work and live right. I believed, in some strange way, a job would be my proof that I was a new person in Christ. Old things had passed away and all things were being made new.

Finally about a week later, I heard about a job opening in a tire warehouse. Once I had filled out my application, I negotiated about my pay. It seemed that they hadn't really decided on the proper hourly wage for someone to sling tires from one side of the warehouse to another and load tires on to a truck. After some going back and forth, we settled on five dollars an hour. I came in every morning to the tire store and was taken to a warehouse to work all day along with a couple of other men. One week later, I was feeling pretty good about myself. After all these years, I was a changed man. I was a productive citizen in the community. I went to church that Sunday and rested that evening. I watched a little TV and turned in early for the night so I could get up Monday morning to begin another week on my new job. I arrived bright and early that Monday morning, rested and ready to go to work.

I was almost at the door when my supervisor said, "Mr. Longcrier, I would like to speak with you in my office in a few minutes. Why don't you just have a seat. Get yourself a cup of coffee while you're waiting. We'll call you in a few minutes."

I wondered what it could be. Maybe they've noticed how hard I've been working and want to give me a raise. Maybe they want to discuss moving me to a better position. Surely I could do some other job besides working in the warehouse.

Minutes later, they called me in the office with my supervisor standing and a man sitting behind a desk wearing a white shirt and a tie. The man behind the desk said, "Mr. Longcrier, we've just had a chance to process your application, we see that you are a convicted felon. I'm afraid that our policy does not allow us to hire felons. I'm sorry, we have to let you go."

I was extremely disappointed. How could this happen when I was trying so hard to live right?

26

GOOD SAMARITANS AND CHURCH FOLK

One evening while I was eating supper with Aunt Bea, the phone rang. It was Marvin Zerden, the owner of Zerden's Men's Store, a long-time presence in downtown Hickory. Zerden's Men's Store was one of the many places I applied in my search for work. "Mr. Longcrier, do you have any experience in men's clothes?" he asked.

"Yes, sir," I answered.

"Where have you worked before?"

When I said, "Atlantic City, Washington D.C., and New York," I really wasn't fibbing because I did have experience in selling men's clothes. I left out the part about them being hot or stolen. I couldn't tell Mr. Zerden that if I really wanted the job! I told him I was a good salesman, figuring if I could sell fake watches and rings, I could sell clothes with my gift of gab.

Mr. Zerden said, "Mr. Longcrier, can you report for work here on Saturday morning at nine?"

"Yes, sir!" was my ready reply.

Saturday morning, I was up bright and early, ready for work. I ate a good breakfast and was ready to start walking. When I stepped out of the door, the woman who usually took me to the Adventist church on Saturday morning was just pulling up to the curb. I walked over to the car to tell her that I wouldn't be coming to church with her this morning because I got a job starting that morning. Judging from the look on her face, she seemed annoyed and disappointed at my news. She reminded me that Saturday was the Sabbath, the Sabbath was to be kept holy, and that I should know better. I told her that I did know better. I reminded her that there was a synagogue ruler who had been disappointed with Jesus for having worked on the Sabbath day by healing a woman who had suffered with an infirmity for eighteen years. Jesus reminded them that on the Sabbath day, they led their oxen from the stall to water them. I told her that my ox was in the stall and I needed to work to get it out.

I said, "I'm going to work for Jewish people and their Sabbath day is Saturday also. These people have run a successful retail business working on Saturday for more than fifty years. They seem to be doing pretty good by God, giving someone like me a chance. Maybe they know something about God and the Sabbath that some people haven't learned yet."

The woman pulled off, screeching rubber before I had a chance to ask her for a ride to work. I would have to walk fast to make up for the time I wasted talking. I wanted to get to work bright and early on my first day to make a good impression. It was ten minutes to nine when I arrived at the store. I wanted to arrive earlier but considering I had to walk, at least I was on time.

Mr. Zerden greeted me at the door and handed me a card to fill out with my name, address, phone number, date of birth, age, and social security number. When I finished, I handed the card back to Mr. Zerden. He introduced me to his son-in-law Al, his wife Elaine, and his sister Ester. I did not know then how special these people would become to me in the years that followed. Mr. Zerden walked me around the first floor of the store showing me how the merchandise was arranged. On the left side of the store were dress suits in regular sizes. Big and tall sizes were at the back of the store along with the shoes. On the right in the front of the store, he showed me where to find the sweaters and men's casual shirts. In the middle aisles were dress slacks ranging from sizes twenty-eight to sixty. Suites and sports coats were in the back to the right. Blue jeans, tennis shoes, coats, and jackets were downstairs. Now that I had been upstairs and downstairs with a pretty good idea where everything was located, I was ready to do some selling! Mr. Zerden put his arm around my shoulder and walked me to the back of the store. He handed me a vacuum cleaner and asked me to vacuum the whole store from top to bottom. When I finished that, he took me to the sweaters and asked me to fold them neatly according to size. Then I did the same with the jeans, the dress slacks, and the shirts.

Occasionally when a customer came in, he would ask me to stop what I was doing to wait on them. If I made a sale, I would bring them to the counter so Ester or one of the others could ring the items up. In the weeks to come, it was pretty much the same routine day in and day out. I was anxious to sell. I knew I could sell and make some good sales. I later realized that I really didn't know anything about selling compared to Al and Ester. They had mastered the art of selling. If a man came in to buy a belt, they could convince him to buy a new pair of slacks and shirt to match. If someone came in to buy a shirt, they would sell them a sport coat and pair of dress slacks to match. If someone came in to buy a black suit, they would end up leaving with a black suit, a brown suit, a blue suit, and shirts and ties to match. Sometimes I brought customers to the counter thinking they had all that they were going to buy. Ester would take them downstairs and come back up with an armful of stuff to go along with the stuff they were already buying.

Sometimes they saw me struggling to make a sale. When it looked like I might lose the customer, they would step in and complete the sale. It didn't take me long to realize that what I thought I knew about selling was nothing compared to what this family knew. In addition to learning how to sell, I learned some valuable lessons about life, people, family, and other things from them. Mr. Zerden became a surrogate father who mentored and counseled me in everything from sales to politics. We loved to share a good joke and enjoyed laughing together. It became such a regular part of our day that his wife Elaine would say, "Reggie, what new joke are you and Mr. Zerden laughing about today?"

I learned quickly. In less than a year, my sales had increased and I was allowed to handle money, sometimes even closing out the register at night. Like the Apostle Paul, I had learned to be content with $4.50 an hour and biweekly paychecks. I worked six days a week and was in church every Sunday.

I did not tell Mr. Zerden everything about my past but I was afraid that someone else would sooner or later. Once I had established a track record for being a good worker who was honest and trustworthy, I decided to roll out bits and pieces of my past to Mr. Zerden. I tried not to overwhelm him for fear he would become distrustful of me before he got to know the new person I was becoming. Every now and then, a customer would see me working there and pull Mr. Zerden aside to whisper something about me. People who heard I was working for Mr. Zerden would walk through the store to see if it was true. Some of my old hustling friends would travel from distant cities to see if fast-living Reggie Longcrier had really changed his life.

One day, I was standing near the front entrance of the store and looking out the window. I saw a woman I knew who was a Christian—or I thought she was because she attended church every Sunday. Her nephew and I had been friends before in prison. I decided to step out of the store to speak to her since I had not seen her for years. I thought that since she was a Christian, she would be glad to hear that I turned my life around.

"Hello, Mrs. Mary," I said.

She turned around, recognized me, and said "Reggie, is that you?"

"Yes, ma'am," I answered.

She asked, "How have you been?"

"Fine, ma'am."

"You really look nice."

"Thank you, ma'am." We made small talk about her nephew.

Once we had gotten past the preliminaries, she looked me up and down. Then she looked behind me into the store. "What are you doing here?" she asked.

I said, "I work here now. I've been working here for almost a year now."

"Wait a minute!" she said, "You mean to tell me that they let you work in this store?" She then began to shake her head in disbelief, mumbling, "Um, they must not know who they got working for them."

I said, "Ma'am, I'm not like I used to be. I've changed." I told her that the last time I was in prison, I turned my life over to the Lord and I had been working ever since I got out. I explained that I was in church every Sunday. I thought she would be happy at hearing the good news. Maybe she would shout and say, "Praise the Lord!"

Instead, she seemed annoyed at what she had heard. She began to shake her head back and forth and said, "No, no, no, no! I knew I shouldn't have stopped to talk to you. I've got to go now. I don't want to hear no more from you. You ain't changed."

I was hurt and surprised at how she responded. This was certainly not the reaction that I had expected from a Christian woman who attended church every Sunday. Once I composed myself, I said, "Well, the Lord saved you, didn't he?"

She said, "Yeah, but that's different."

I said, "Maybe I've misjudged you. I thought since you were in church every Sunday, you would understand."

She walked away mumbling something under her breath. That day was the beginning of my education in how hurtful and insensitive so-called Christians could be. I met other so-called Christians who viewed my new faith in God with the same type of suspicion. They acted like they thought I had some new trick up my sleeve. Even some of my kinsfolk were leery of my faith and, at times, didn't mind me hearing them say so.

Who do you talk to besides God when the people who are supposed to support you are the ones hurting you the most? I thank God for Mr. Jim and Mr. Orders, the two Christian prison ministry volunteers I met during my incarceration. They were the most authentic Christians I had known during my time in prison. They were good for me. I needed their friendship, their counsel, and their support. They taught me how a Christian handles hurt, fear, gossip, and rejection. They kept their cool. Although I considered myself to be a born-again Christian, I had never been in the church culture. I had no idea I would be met with so much suspicion, rejection, and prejudice when I finally wanted to live right. Church folk would say, "We better keep our eye on him. You know he's been to prison. He ain't gonna be nothing. He ain't gonna be no preacher, He can't preach to me."

Trying to be accepted into the culture of the church was like going through a hazing to join a college fraternity. At that time, I could only talk to a handful of white prison ministry volunteers who were trying to help me the best they could. They never invited me to their churches, except on rare occasions. I thought it was because they knew their churches would not be receptive to a black ex-convict as a new member. Even so, they helped me any way that they could. Their kindness and support showed me what true Christians were like.

Mr. Orders had me speak on his thirty-minute radio show every Sunday afternoon at two. I looked forward to this every week. One afternoon, Mr. Orders introduced me to an elderly black woman named Reverend Leander Austin who was the pastor of a small church called People's Tabernacle in Lenoir, North Carolina. She came on the air after we did. Mr. Orders told her about me and how I came out of the prison. He suggested that she invite me to her church to speak. She turned to me and asked, "Would you come to my church next Sunday and say a word?"

"Yes, ma'am!" I answered.

That next Sunday, Mr. Orders drove me to Lenoir to Reverend Austin's church. The service had already begun with a small choir of eight members singing "Amazing Grace" along with the congregation. Pastor Austin and three of her ministers were in the pulpit praising the Lord. Mr. Orders and I sat on the first pew. She got up and said how glad she was to see us there that morning. She talked about how long she had known Mr. Orders, what a good man he was, and the good work he was doing in the prison ministry. Then she looked at me and said, "I met this remarkable young man with Mr. Orders at the radio station last week. I would like for him to come up and say a word."

I was green and thought when she said that she wanted me to "say a word" that she meant for me to preach a message. I didn't know any better so I walked into this woman's pulpit, opened my Bible to Luke 15:11, and began preaching about the prodigal son. I wove bits and pieces of my testimony through the message. Coming to the end, all the congregation could do was say, "Amen. Praise the Lord!"

Ministers who sat in the pulpit with Pastor Alston, who probably waited months for their turn to preach, were confused by what I had done. This seasoned pastor who had served more than forty years in the pulpit managed her surprise with a nod and a grin. She stood, commented on my message, and led the altar call and final prayer. Poor Mr. Orders. He didn't know any better either so he kept running around, praising the Lord, and hugging everyone.

Pastor Austin came to me later and said, "Boy, I didn't mean for you to preach. I was just asking you to give your testimony!" I was so embarrassed. I should have known better. I think she could tell by the look on my face that I really didn't know any better. She threw her arms around me, gave me a big hug, and said, "But you did good!"

Mr. Orders heard what she had said and came over to ask Pastor Austin if she would help me. I told her that he believed God was calling me to be a preacher and he had been trying his best to help me since I was released from prison. He told her I needed to be in a church where I could grow and that he would sacrifice going to his own church to bring me to her church every Sunday. Pastor Austin said she would be glad to help me if Mr. Orders could get me to Lenoir every Sunday. One week later, I joined People's Tabernacle Church. Mr. Orders was faithful to take me every Sunday morning. Pastor Austin became my spiritual mentor and pastor. She nurtured me, guided me, counseled me, promoted me, and supported me everywhere I went. When I would go to a prison to speak, she would go along. When I would speak at a church, she would be there. Pastor Austin trained me in proper pulpit etiquette and exposed me to a wise fellowship of male and female clergy. She taught me many valuable lessons that could not be learned in any seminary classroom. I did not realize what an imprint she made on my life until years later when she went home to be with the Lord. At the time, I didn't realize that she was an angel who walked with me during a season in my life when I needed it most.

During this time, Mr. Orders faithfully drove me wherever I needed to go to speak in churches, prisons, and civic groups, never asking for anything in return. Some churches would take up an offering for me, and I would offer something to Mr. Orders but he would always turn me down. He said, "The Lord wants me to help you until you are self-sufficient." When he said that, I could tell he really believed I would be self-sufficient someday. His confidence in me helped me believe it too. Sometimes when I was struggling to make it from one paycheck to the next and feeling desperate, Mr. Orders would call and say, "Reggie, have you looked in the mail box today? We had a pretty good week, I left you a little something in the mailbox."

I would go to the mailbox to find an envelope with two crisp twenty-dollar bills. He did this on many occasions until I was able to stand on my own. This helped me make the transition from hustling where I got paid every day to working and getting a paycheck every two weeks.

27

FROM DISGRACE
TO DIGNITY

M r. Orders, Mr. Jim, and Pastor Austin had me busy speaking in some jail, prison, or church almost every weekend. On the fourth Sunday of every month, I would go to Catawba Correctional Center in Newton, North Carolina, along with Mr. Goforth and Mr. Orders to conduct the nine worship service. I got to know Mr. Goforth and Mr. Orders while I was an inmate in this prison and regularly attended those Sunday morning services when they came in to minister to us. Now I was just as dedicated as they were in coming into minister to men who sat where I used to sit.

My comeback testimony of resurrection was a good message many people wanted to hear. Inmates wanted to hear it because it gave them hope to see that someone like me could change. My change was indisputable evidence that God is real. I never knew when my message might fall on the ears of one who was ready to change so I was passionate about going into the prisons as often as I could. When speaking in churches or civic groups, I knew that a parent, grandparent, sister, brother, husband, or wife needed the hope that it was not too late for their loved one. The same God that had done it for me could do it for them too. Doors began opening for me and soon I was speaking in prisons all over the state. I was earning a good reputation in prison ministry that a man named Ron Spencer asked me if I would be interested in serving on the board of the Community Resource Council and Catawba Prison Ministries. The resource council and prison ministry worked together in collaboration as a liaison between the community and the prison. I knew Mr. Spencer from the Sunday school class that he taught for many years at Catawba Correctional Center. Mr. Spencer was also the chairman of the resource council. He had a lot of faith in me and believed I would be a good board member. All resource council members had to be approved by the governor. Some people didn't know whether or not the governor would appoint an ex-convict to the Community Resource Council. Ron Spencer was determined to nominate me for the board and submitted my name along with letters of recommendation. After some time passed, I received a letter from North Carolina Governor Jim Martin approving me to serve on the board of the Community Resource Council. I was the first ex-convict approved by the governor to serve on the board. It was a big deal to me so I took my responsibilities seriously.

At this time, I was still working for Mr. Zerden who had become my Good Samaritan. One day, I asked him to help me get a car because I had been walking almost a mile each way to and from work because I didn't like depending on other people to take me where I needed to go otherwise. I felt like my need for help with transportation was getting on people's nerves. I told Mr. Zerden that he could deduct money from my paycheck until I paid off the loan. He asked me if I had picked out a car. I told him that I saw a car on a used car lot in downtown Hickory. He offered to go with me to the car lot at lunch time, and we rode together in his car.

I got out of his car, walked over to the used car that I saw, and said, "This is the car I was telling you about." He walked around the car, looked in it, checked under the hood, and asked the salesman to crank it up. He talked awhile with the salesman. I was waiting for him to write the man a check for the car. Instead, he did something else that would help me further down the road in years to come. He was a businessman and knew that I needed to build a credit history because I didn't have one. A man without a credit history is like a king without a thrown or a man marked with an *X*.

We got back in his car, and he took me to his bank to introduce me to one of the branch managers, Mr. Henry Kyzer, who also become a mentor and guide later in my life. "Henry, this is Reggie Longcrier, the fellow I was telling you about who works for me. I want you to fix him up with a loan for this car that he wants. Let him pay it back any way he wants to. If you need me for anything, I will be in my office." He turned and walked out, leaving me in the office with Mr. Kyzer.

Once he had gotten all the paperwork together, he asked me how I had wanted to pay the loan back. This all happened so fast I hardly had time to gather my thoughts! I regained my composure and asked hesitantly, "One hundred dollars a month?"

I was afraid he would say that it wasn't enough. I was surprised to hear him say "Okay." I was even more surprised when he handed me a check for the car to take to the car dealer. Up until now, I had not been used to banks giving me money. I had been used to taking money from banks! It felt so good to be trusted. When I took the check to the dealer for the car, he looked at it for a minute and said, "For this kind of money, they must want a lien on the title." I told him that I didn't know about that and he should call Mr. Kyzer at First Union Bank to see if there should be a lien or not.

After he talked with Mr. Kyzer, he hung up the phone with a puzzled look on his face. "I can't believe this. They told me to let you keep your own title."

Once again, it felt good to be trusted. I had no intentions of betraying the trust that so many good people were giving me. After I paid the car off, I had established good credit. This led to many other credit opportunities, which resulted in me getting other cars and even purchased a home. My life was forever changed because Mr. Zerden took a chance and believed in me. Because he believed in me, I could believe in myself. It gave me hope that I really could do better. I could believe I was somebody. I could believe I didn't have to go back to prison. I could believe I didn't need drugs and didn't need to hustle anymore. Most importantly, I could believe that God is able to supply all of my needs according to his glorious riches.

Now that I had transportation, I traveled throughout the state speaking in prisons and churches. I faithfully served as a volunteer at Catawba Correctional Center with Mr. Orders, Mr. Goforth, and Mr. Spencer. They mentored me ever since my release from prison. A year later, I heard they were looking for a prison chaplain at Catawba Correctional Center. I began to toy with the idea of being a prison chaplain. As quickly as those thoughts came, they vanished into thin air. I didn't want to fool myself. I knew that they would never accept someone with my record. I was an ex-drug addict and an ex-drug dealer. I served time there as an inmate. They would probably want locked me up just for having the audacity to submit an application. I was grateful that I was allowed speak in the prison and help them with their reentry program.

One night, I got a strange phone call from Mr. Spencer. He was part of the chaplain's advisory committee, which was called to help select a chaplain for Catawba Correctional

Center. This group had thirteen clergy from the Lutheran, Episcopal, Baptist, Methodist, Pentecostal, Catholic, Presbyterian, and AME Zion denominations along with regional chaplain, Mr. Ervin Hopkins. Mr. Spencer called me that night to say that someone mentioned I might be interested in the prison chaplain position at the prison.

When I heard this, I thought, *Who could have told him that?* I dared utter a word to anyone that I was even mildly interested in it for fear people would laugh at me just for mentioning it. I said, "Ron, flesh and blood could not have revealed that to you. Only God in heaven could have given you that thought because I dared not mention it to anyone."

He said to me, "Reggie, why don't you just submit your application and see what happens? Let me be honest with you too. We were told to reach high on the totem pole for people who had degrees over past experience. You would be at the bottom of the totem pole."

I reluctantly submitted my application with the prodding of Mr. Spencer. When the day of decision came, they had twelve applicants for the job. All were armed to the teeth with the proper credentials, degrees, and experience—all except me. Two of the pastors on the advisory committee brought their associate pastors in for the job. I was definitely at the bottom of the totem pole. Each applicant went on the hot seat to be questioned and sized up by the advisory board. They asked many questions such as, "How do you feel about Muslims? Could you minister to them? What about gay inmates? Could you minister to them? What about salvation? What about using Scripture?" They posed different scenarios. "What would you do if an inmate came to you with a life-threatening situation? How would you build relationships with inmates?"

I was very comfortable in the interview because being in a prison setting is something I understood well. I was the only candidate who had lived on both sides of the situation. I knew how to show them the inside of an inmate's incarceration experience and how a chaplain could be most helpful. It was easy to show them how inmates view chaplains versus the prison administration and what we need to do to gain their trust. I have always been open-minded and had no problems with any of the diversity questions. Who am I to judge anyone? My answers were in-depth and thoughtful. I felt like I had done my best, the rest was up to God. All the applicants had their time before the panel, and it was time for them to vote on their decision. By the grace and favor of God, they voted unanimously and unequivocally. I was the new chaplain at Catawba Correctional Center! I still had one more hurdle to overcome because I had to be approved by the Community Resource Council and the prison superintendent.

The next week, I met with the chaplain's advisory committee and the Community Resource Council at the prison for final approval. When I arrived at the prison that morning, I had to wait in the programmer's office while they made their decision in the inmate dining hall a few yards away. Within five minutes, they sent for me to come to the dining hall. As I approached the entrance, they were coming out of the dining hall giving me smiles and nods of approval. They said, "You're the chaplain now, you got the job! We've got good news and bad news. The good news is you got it. The bad news is that we don't have any money to pay you."

They didn't know I was glad to do the job for nothing. As a matter of fact, I did the job for nothing for close to a year while we raised money from churches throughout Catawba county. Mr. Spencer and I went to just about every church's Sunday school, men's breakfast, Wednesday night meetings, Bible study, or Sunday morning worship service seeking support for Catawba Prison Ministries, the nonprofit created to employ the chaplain and provide services in the prison. Every week, Mr. Spencer and I were speaking at a local church or civic organization. We raised money for the chaplain's budget and funds for a future chapel on the grounds of the prison. At that time, our worship services were held in a small trailer on the grounds of the prison or we worshiped occasionally in the inmate dining hall in the midst of the pots and pans clinging and clanging as they were washed. After a year, we had enough money in the budget to pay me for twenty hours a week, although I was consistently giving thirty-five hours a week or more while still holding down a full time job at Zerdens Men's Store. Every night, an officer escorted me to the gate to let me out so I could go home. Going in and out of the prison like this was rather strange for a man who had spent so many years incarcerated. Even stranger than that was the fact that I was the chaplain despite my record. I am living proof that with God all things are possible.

Sometimes when I got to the prison, rain would be pouring down. I would pick up the phone outside the gate to let someone know I was waiting to be let in. I would hear the officers laughing over the intercom. After a long time, I would hear, "We need a yard officer to let the chaplain in at the front gate." Sometime later, an officer would stroll up to the gate with an umbrella over his head, taking his time while torrents of rain were coming down. The gate would open and the officer escorted me to my office to unlock the door because they had not given me a key to my own office. Six months later, I got a key to my office.

Soon after I became chaplain, an officer was escorting me to the gate to let me out. As we walked to the gate, he asked me how I was getting along and if I liked the job as chaplain. Before I could answer him, he said, "If I had my way, I would line them all up on the wall and shoot them."

I responded, "Officer, I'm surprised to hear you say that because people like me would have no chance. If it had been left up to you, I would never be chaplain here. I've served time in prison. As a matter of fact, I've served time in this prison. Did you tell the people who hired you here how you felt? Maybe you're working in the wrong place."

He put his head down in shame and apologized, "I was just running off at the mouth and didn't really mean anything by it."

I got the best training a prison chaplain could ever want because some of the most experienced chaplains from all over North Carolina came and spent time nurturing and training me. They had a vested interest in my success. Chaplain Bud Walker, the chaplain coordinator for the state sent the first check supporting me as chaplain. He came to visit me from time to time, giving me nuggets of wisdom. Chaplain Frank Shirley, the regional chaplain coordinator, would send me material through the prison bus mail, call me every week, and come to take me to lunch at least once a month. Chaplain Shirley had been my chaplain while I was serving time in Craggy prison in the North Carolina mountains. He would have his chaplain meetings for the chaplains in the western region once a month at the Little Vienna Restaurant in Marion, North Carolina. We would meet to learn and fellowship with other chaplains serving prisons in the western region.

Every three months, Chaplain Shirley would come to Hickory and pick me up along with other chaplains in one of the state vans to go to Raleigh for our statewide chaplain's meeting. We would usually check into the hotel that evening, eat together, fellowship, and then get up the next morning to attend the statewide meeting. On the way back, we would stop for ice cream, and the fellowship was always great. Khalil Akbar, the Islamic coordinator for the state over ninety-six prisons would come to see me at least once a month and take me to lunch. This time together was priceless and always edifying. Lincolnton chaplain Mickey Champion and Allen Carpenter from the Dallas prison would sometimes leave their prison to come check in on me at my unit. Chaplain Jim Osborne was jokingly called the "Bishop of Chaplains" because he held the chaplain positions at two prisons, Huntersville and Mecklenburg. Chaplain Osborne came often, offering to help me in spite of his busy schedule.

The tireless dedication of these men taught me the seriousness of the call of ministry and that our work was not to be taken lightly. Despite all they had poured into me, I still yearned for more. I felt a bit handicapped because I was the only chaplain who had been to prison. I needed something more to help ease my insecurity so I enrolled in the American chaplain training program at Mulligan College in Johnson City, Tennessee. This program was the only one of its kind. I studied with the brilliant Tom Beckner, one of the leading authors on prison chaplaincy in the county. I spent two weeks on the campus of Mulligan College along with other chaplains who came from all over the country from as far away as Alaska. We bonded, fellowshipped, and learned at the feet of this giant who shared his wisdom with us. On graduation day, we took pictures, exchanged addresses, and said our goodbyes. I realized then that education would be an ongoing endeavor.

Once I got back to North Carolina, I hit the ground running, working in the men's clothing store during the day and spending time at the prison in the evenings. Sometimes the inmates would tease me because I was at the prison so much. "Man, why don't you just take a bunk and spend the night?"

I was called to Raleigh to be officially commissioned as a prison chaplain for the state of North Carolina along with other chaplains who were being commissioned that year. This was a very proud moment in my life and another milestone on my road to recovery. When I had been chaplain for a year and half, the superintendent of the prison handed me the keys to prison gate so I could come in and out on my own. This meant more to me than all of the great things that had happened since I walked out of prison as an inmate for the last time. It was the most significant accomplishment of all. Holding the keys to the prison gate was the symbol of my journey from disgrace to dignity. The road had been paved with so much pain. It had passed through dreams of success that became nightmares of illusion where my name was replaced for a number and my wardrobe became a uniform. What I thought would bring me status only brought me shame and disgrace.

I never dreamed I would be a prison chaplain. Only God could take a crooked road and make it straight. Only God could take a convict and transform him into a prison chaplain. God took my failure and gave me amazing grace. I had a new life with a loving God who made it possible for me to hold my foot in the door for so many others who need another chance to live again.

EPILOGUE

Through many dangers, toils, and
snares, I have already come.

—John Newton

After going through the maze of addiction, incarceration, and foolish living, I finally made it out. Scores of others are still running around in the same maze like mice looking for fake cheese. Some may never find their way out. If this is you, listen to the still small voice inside that is trying to help you learn the lessons life has been trying to teach you. You don't have to keep making the same mistakes over and over again. You don't have to keep falling in the same traps time after time. God is real and God can help you.

For all those who read this book, God has done much more than give me the keys to the prison gate where I was once an inmate. I have been the chaplain of Catawba Correctional Center since 1989. This is just one of the miracles God worked in my life.

We would love to hear from you about how this book blessed you or the ones you love. My contact information is below.

Rev. Reggie Longcrier
revlongcrier@exodushomes.org
P.O. Box 3311
Hickory, North Carolina 28603
www.catawbaprisonministries.org
www.exodusmissionaryoutreachchurch.org
www.exodushomes.org

ABOUT THE AUTHOR

Reverend Reggie Longcrier has been the chaplain of Catawba Correctional Center in Newton, North Carolina, since 1989. He is a national public speaker in correctional institutions (including death row), churches, human services agencies, conferences, and other settings. His testimony of recovery from twenty-five years of heroin addiction and incarceration give him extraordinary credibility as a leader in this field. *From Disgrace to Dignity* tells the story of his amazing transformation.

Reverend Longcrier founded Exodus Missionary Outreach Church in 1997, a nondenominational, multi-ethnic congregation in Hickory, North Carolina. Exodus church (www.exodusmissionaryoutreachchurch.org) has grown rapidly and gained an outstanding reputation for its diversity, inclusiveness, and innovative approach for reaching those typically left back by mainstream churches.

In 1998, Reverend Longcrier became the founding executive director of Exodus Homes (www.exodushomes.org), a faith-based United Way organization in Hickory that provides transitional to long-term supportive housing for homeless recovering people who are returning to the community from treatment centers and prisons. Exodus Homes has sixty-three beds with eight program locations in Hickory with a comprehensive continuum of services to meet the needs of its residents including in-house enterprises called Exodus Works, which create jobs for its residents. The success of Exodus Homes has earned the program a national reputation that goes all the way to the White House.

Over the years, Reverend Longcrier has won many awards and is a tireless advocate for equality and justice for all people in our society.